CW00523549

GIRDERS IN THE SAND

GIRDERS IN THE SAND

John Marr

© January 2000. *Exile*

First published in Great Britain by *Exile*.
1 Armstrong Close, Hundon, Suffolk, CO10 8HD.

e-mail: exile@2from.com.

©John Marr 2000

All rights reserved. This book is sold subject to the conditions that it shall not, by way of trade or otherwise, be lent, re-sold, hired out or otherwise circulated without the publisher's prior consent in any form of binding or cover other than that in which it is published and without a similar condition including this condition being imposed on the subsequent purchaser. No part of this publication may be reproduced, stored in a retrieval system, or transmitted, in any form or by any means, electronic, mechanical, photocopying, recording or otherwise, without prior permission of the publishers and copyright holders except by way of critical review or academic study for purposes of quotation only.

ISBN 0-9537917-1-8

Printed in Great Britain by Proprint, Stibbington, Cambs.

Always longing to confound those cynics who believe Art and Science to be incompatible, John Marr, then a GP in a busy practice, quit his comfortable lifestyle to begin a quest which would take him fifteen years. How much this epic work reflects his own life is not known by even his closest freinds. *Girders in the Sand* was taken from a dream; with a life-long love of poetry, he struggled to complete it, taking an Msc in cosmology the better to understand our origins.

An old boy of St Thomas' Hospital, designer of Zillian, the first world champion table tennis robot, and co-editor of a poetry magazine, he is living proof that Art and Science share a common bond.

To Ann - the power behind the pen.

Contents

Prologue

O power, beyond the mind of puny men,
　　That stirs our hearts to leave the well-worn ways
　　For travel through some distant, trackless fen–
　　　Though yet unhallowed grave may end our days–
Now let us move from darkest, hidden birth.
False recollections of great, former times
May draw us back; but, as with mother Earth–
Which forged from minute minutes season's rhymes:
Raw spring, bold summer, now autumnal gold
To glitter and allure enfeebled mind–
Like Earth, so we must spawn a child to hold
Ere winter's kiss leaves naught but frost behind.

　　　This universal story each man knows
　　　Which, constant in retelling, constant grows.

* * * * *

　　　Our scene unfolds now: different climes,
　　　Peopled through such far flung times
　　　　　As make a universe.
　　　Yet all compacted in one span:
　　　Breath of but a single man,
　　　　　Who grows to this discourse.

1

Edwin-Son

So this is he, young Edwin-son:
One not of any noble birth,
Unrefined, undignified,
      And lacking even manly stance;
He tried his hand at factory jobs,
Drilling templates by the gross–
Steel plates to line some nuclear flues,
But did not care to be so used.
With aching arm and throbbing head
He left to idle time alone.
But parents who themselves worked hard
Were only keen to see him paired.
They said that, "Independent he
Must from henceforth suffice to be!"
And work like they to earn his keep;
His schooling done, he'd better see
About the business of the world.
He wrote, and got another job,
Pulling pennies week by week,
He sweated daily in a shop
Trying sorely to persuade
Heavy maids to petite shoes,
Using oily repartee
To urge them take accessories-
Those fancy polishes and hose
And cloths to rub their shiny shoes
To coax them shine till, like the news,
They had to be discarded.
For nothing grates more on the mind
Than footwear of a former kind,
Especially so when friends comment
That they have seen that pair before.

Prologue

Thus trade was brisk, Edwin did well:
To under-manager he rose.

But then began his sorest woes—
For in this post of heady height,
He had to strive to sell yet more
By setting targets for his staff;
And they must daily each compete
One with another for the feet
Of clients by rushing to the door
And pulling in the women there
To urge them buy without a care,
Whatever fashions of the day
Were best to pump his profits up.
Those girls who did not make the grade
Were quickly sacked— 'twas only trade!
No matter if they chums had been;
And many a long, low look he earned
From former friends whose love he spurned.
No! Mighty profit was his aim,
His rule, his life, his mistress too:
Ten charts he took home and arrayed
In technicolour round his room.
To see the graphs and lines rise high
Made him warm and glow within.
He went on courses, learnt the trade;
Each weekly circular received
Showed well their placing relative
To other stores. He had to climb,
To hump his shop up to the top;
For he among the middle men
Could never be content to stay.
Yet e'er elusive was that goal-
That prime-most site as head of all.
His manager grew crosser then,

Girders in the Sand

And ranted, "You must spur them on!
They've promised me a trip abroad
(And with my wife) if from this horde
Of rivals I can soon attain
The top-most rank! Now play the game!"
Edwin did try. He'd learnt the rules;
One girl named Jane, who had done well,
Now sadly slipped– statistically–
Until she hardly sold a shoe.
He called her in, then bawled her out.
She cried in anguish drops so large
They fell and smudged his sales returns.
She looked so young and pretty too,
And yet she had a child of two;
But by this Edwin was not swayed.
He made her leave, though part dismayed
By what he'd done. And in her place
He took a younger training girl
Who could be given half the wage
And be dismissed within three months
If she by then no promise showed.

Edwin did well; he rose in turn
To manage one store on his own.
But when he fain reached dizzy height
By lying third in all the land,
He was admonished out of hand
For not yet being top-most kite.
For other shops adjacent were,
Which figures proved had sold yet more.
Hence Edwin was spurred further on-
To do them down and force a loss
In their returns. It seemed unfair.
How could he guide girls what to wear?
He couldn't drag them from the street

Prologue

To help adorn their dainty feet.
He chose instead a call to make,
Across the road to see this store
Whose sales returns were so much more.
Strange chance! The manager he knew,
Prior to coming here to shoe.
A man called Stan; they'd shared a school,
Aye, not so many years before,
And soon to chatting they bestirred:
Of common past, and of their load
In life. Ere long, Stan slyly showed
Circulars from Head Office.
The names were different at the top,
But that apart they fair agreed
With every line on Edwin's screed.
Even the date was thus alike:
Wednesday, the First of June. How odd.
They pondered this o'er mid-day beer
And sandwiches at their local,
The aptly named 'Black Anvil'.
For Edwin's shop, it seemed, like Stan's,
Was owned by huge conglomerate
Named 'British Shoe'. That was a fact,
But so it seemed were other stores:
Full half a dozen in their town;
Indeed, that number lined one street.
It looked as though 'most half the feet
In England were thus shod the same:
They differed but in label name.
Bemused and tired they wandered back,
Each to compete with each the more
At limited resources' door.

Girders in the Sand

Edwin had never thought before
Of deeper things– what life was for;
Why he remorselessly must strive
Against his friends to keep alive;
Why sweat to make his shop the best,
When other shops across the street
Were likewise aiming to compete
For self-same lucre from the feet
Of women wishing to look neat.
So many people selling shoes;
Straining their guts out to sell more,
Girl 'gainst girl and store 'gainst store,
All for a pittance! For he saw
They little gained from all this toil–
It hardly seemed to pay their rent.
They most were single, or filled time
Augmenting Saturday's brisk trade
By coming then to lend support
To his more regular young crew
Who profit generate. He knew
Just how much money could accrue
From selling boots or leather shoe.
All their labour– ill expended–
Fed one small group at the peak,
And they most likely dwelt abroad;
For he had heard this Titan horde
Had other empires 'cross the lands:
New York, Geneva, Paris, Rome,
There seemed no end to what they owned.
His brain was reeling, pondering thus,
And inwardly he cursed them all
That made him puppet to their call.
But yet, he had a job to do:
He went on fitting madam's shoe.

The Betrothal of Edwin

Edwin now moved through melancholy times;
Long days were punctuated by poor sleep
And dreaded work, as if some heinous crimes
Were perpetrated, though all rules he'd keep.
One friend who caught him thus sought to advise,
"I take each day the juice of one orange–
For see, this vitamin should make me wise;
Alternatively, suck health on a lozenge!"
Another, quick to heed his psyche sore stressed,
And lacking greater conversational ploy,
Advised him, part serious, yet part in jest,
To marry; hoping like a child's new toy
That such distractions might soon quench his fires.
(But married men were ever the worst liars.)

* * * * *

Edwin then took a subtle turn,
Which weakness failed to discern–
And called itself 'Romance'.
While still distracted by his life,
He sought comfort with a wife–
And fell to love's soft dance.

Girders in the Sand

About this time it happened that
A new girl started on the floor;
Young and pretty, full of joy,
She captivated Edwin-son
Who wooed her daily, brushing hands
And touching hair until she fell
To his sad looks; so debonair
In smart lounge suit, with matching shoes
(Obtained at discount from his store).

This lively lass helped run a troupe
Of guides, and of them justly proud.
With selfless heart and gentle ways
She cherished music, and its strains
Ran through her life; she wished to learn
Mastery of the soulful cello.
Having left her school behind,
She took this job just for some fun
Of earning money of her own.
Their lightening courtship amazed all:
Within a month he had proposed;
They'd found a place and time to wed;
All were invited– bride and groom,
Their families and friends; the church
Set up and flowered through for show.
The vicar 'vised indulgently,
But with their haste had to agree:
For when two loved as these two did,
It should be shared and never hid.
And Joy, named as her nature was,
Did love him thus: that she for he
Would e'en forgo her laid-out plans
To stay with Edwin and be wed;
And to this end, within her heart,
She crooned her troth for Edwin-son:

The Betrothal of Edwin

"My love and my delight-
My spring and summer sun-
      I hear you laugh,
      I see you smile-
You I cherish with each while,
My walk's upon your path.

"You are all hope to me-
My being and my life.
      Though but a boy
      With far to go,
My tide of love through you will flow;
In you I will know joy.

"Singing children sound your name;
It whispers in the wind.
      The moving stars,
      The shifting sands,
Are naught to me, while we hold hands
Like pictures on a vase.

"The earth moves round the setting sun;
With change in everything;
      Yet at his knee
      My breath is fanned;
My whole world ends in Edwin's hand:
Through him I shall be free."

The Marriage of Edwin

I

First to bestir itself, a fresh, slow breeze
Slipped through the dying night while all was still
To move the heavy, mist-enshrouded trees
And cleanse the air with ancient, practised skill
Before unfurling plants upon the hill.
Then, through the silence, piped a lonely bird-
The herald of those hordes which soft night kill-
And to his voice uncounted others heard
And joined until, to this grand chorus, sweet Joy stirred.

II

She rose, and like the sun her face shone bright,
(But unlike his, whose incandescence showed
Itself in simple, dull, unchanging light,
Her light grew more as inner feelings flowed,)
To lift her looks till all who saw her glowed
And felt within that living radiancy,
With innocence alike on all bestowed:
As blameless as though locked in infancy
Which, seeing her, brought enmity to clemency.

The Marriage of Edwin

III

The bride was first to wake within the home,
And glad to know a time of quiet bliss
Wherein she moved with measured stealth, alone,
To take her bath, and dream of Edwin's kiss.
Then, leisured thus, she full resolved to miss
Her breakfast, and take cool refreshing air
Within the world outside: that dark abyss
Where lingers yet the livery fools wear
To hide embarrassment of lives so sadly bare.

IV

She gently moved among the long shadows
Cast by the new-up sun which, slanting through
Tall buildings, glistened: as wet grass bestows
A look of diamonds scattered on the dew.
Of other early risers there were few,
And swiftly she slipped through the wood's first hedge
And sensed in there a presence, which she knew
Was in her deepest being: at the edge
Of consciousness; but more than this she could not dredge.

V

On her return, her sister ran to greet,
And cried with mock alarm least she had flown-
Finding too hard the strain of what was meet.
Some final preparations of her own
Must hastily be done: her tresses sewn
With orchids through the veil; her bridal gown
Tried on; some fresh bouquets her mother shown;
And then persuade their father to come down.
At last, the ribboned car arrived to drive to town.

Girders in the Sand

VI

Edwin, meanwhile, with circumspection moved;
He had some doubt that haste-concocted plan
Might not in his best interest yet be proved,
Though Joy he loved– as might so any man.
But marriage– left to him he'd sooner ban!
And yet he loved her, and to please her so,
He packed a case and put it in his van
Then drove with his best friend– though somewhat slow–
Toward the church, his single state there to forego.

VII

He still had time in hand before that hour
Appointed for conjoining seperatehood;
He'd thought to send his love a token flower,
And dwelt on idle thoughts of what they would
Be sharing once the day was done; his blood
Ran sharp until, with hot agitation,
He spied an open pub which looked so good
His friend urged him to show no hesitation,
But drive into the courtyard for sweet oblation.

VIII

They supped a pint or two of best bitter.
Archie– his best man– gladly shared anew:
None knew better how much he could fritter
From his frail life, by drinking hops' good brew.
Time passed until of minutes there were few
Before incestuous time claimed its own hour.
Edwin stirred then, to take vows quaint and true,
But Archie held him back from bridle bower,
With sudden talk that douched his thoughts like a cold
shower.

The Marriage of Edwin

IX

The news that day– as every day!– had told
Of horrid death; but this was near at hand.
A girl had died, just twenty-one years old;
She'd had a child, but they could hardly stand
Through hunger and that deep remorseless brand
Of poverty, though she would ne'er complain–
Until she jumped. Five stories up: she'd planned
Both to be dashed. All thought she was insane.
The child lay in her arms; the mother's name was Jane.

X

The landlord was a rotund, kindly man
Who'd sold his beer for nigh on twenty years.
He'd known Ed's friends when they at first began
To frequent pubs from school for illicit beers;
And seeing Edwin thus wise moved to tears
By what should be but pending nuptial bliss,
He bought a round to stem impending fears
And urged Edwin to nothing take amiss,
But go forth like the man he was, to meet bride's kiss.

XI

Now Edwin, to their chagrin, cried the more,
And vowed he was not fit to take a wife.
The death of Jane had shocked him to the core–
And he took all the guilt for her sad life.
For he'd not only added to her strife
By sacking her, without the means to pay
Her rent or food, but– in his mind more rife–
Were other thoughts of she he'd made obey
His will; how to his love, she'd often been a prey.

Girders in the Sand

XII

For Jane had died; e'en she, whom he'd first loved.
While Archie urged him rise and greet the church,
And mine host cleared the glasses, and mock-cuffed
The lads, and pushed them from their counter-perch,
And said, "no fool would leave Joy in the lurch.
Hurry– or they'll start the opening hymn!"
Edwin felt that a supple, thrashing birch
Was all the sport that should accrue to him.
Dear, gentle Jane, whose trusting eyes now left him grim.

XIII

Low, soft, sombre resonance cleaved the air
And moved funereally with murmur's pace.
The consternation of the guests was clear
As from her loft the organist could place
No meaning in this groomless scene. Like lace
She moved mellisonant fingers 'cross the keys
And thought this was a most unlikely brace
To be soon spliced; so with this time to seize,
Selections from old musicals she chose to please.

XIV

Outside, the bride had circled with papa
On being told that all was not quite set
Until, exasperated in the car,
She strode into the church in fulsome pet
To ask why by her groom she was not met;
And remonstrated there on in-law's side.
But Edwin's mother nothing knew as yet;
"He never really wanted you," she cried.
Poor Joy. She was, in truth, a most unhappy bride.

The Marriage of Edwin

XV

But scarce had Joy indrawn her breath to wail,
Than through the porch with great commotion came
Edwin. He coughed and hurried down the aisle;
The vicar looked so pleased to have his game.
What happened next, do not the organist blame,
But on the vicar's nod she took her cue
And blasted out those chords of bridal fame
Which are fit recompense for maids who woo;
Though all this put Joy's mother in a proper stew.

XVI

The congregation mustered what remained
Of dignity, and hid embarrassment
In *Rock of Ages*, as song-sheet ordained.
Edwin the while, recovering his breath spent
On chasing through the town on marriage bent,
Tried whispering to his bride the dolorous cause,
Like he who brought the news from Aix to Ghent:
But, unlike he who made that town to pause,
Their vicar started reading ancient marriage laws.

XVII

An eagle with spread pinions locked in brass-
Grave aspect of once mighty, living bird-
Now stooped to bear some open, weighty mass
Whose textual sayings- once the living word-
Are now embalmed: unchanging, so unheard,
Cast in leaden ingots through each age
Till so remote that heaven's view is blurred.
And passages that once wrought fervent rage
Now have less impact than young actors on a stage.

Girders in the Sand

XVIII

The couple moved before the alter rail
And stood, with silent expectation's rite,
Agreeing each to each now to impale:
Two disparate bodies fused by solemn might
As shaft and string are joined for arrow's flight;
Or clay and water mixed for potter's vase;
Or earth-bound dreams attain some golden height;
As dust is joined to dust to preform stars
Which soon the gathering mass with fiery brilliance chars.

XIX

Do not assume, in reading this report,
That Edwin's will was weak or that he lacked
Something of character in what he thought
A man should be about. For he had stacked
Against him every habit, neatly packed,
Which, from parents or peers, is fresh acquired:
Each passed on down the centuries, well backed
By ritual custodians, who conspired
In gaudy trappings to grasp what they desired.

XX

You here who read, and reading understand,
Will know the weight traditions have conferred
On language, dress, food, wealth, where we stand-
(In politics or hearth as is preferred).
So great the weight, distinctions become blurred
Between what's done by rote, and what we choose:
As each reply is in the tongue we've heard
At mother's knee- and that we cannot loose-
So other's pre-formed words adorn the thoughts we use.

The Marriage of Edwin

XXI

Take back the painted trappings from the man;
Strip off the silvered face he shows the world;
Peel out the layers of culture which this fan
Of civil form spreads like some flag unfurled
To glorify those bloody wounds men hurled
At men– once named the "Glorious Flag of War"–
Till round their naked viciousness it twirled.
A skirt to hide behind, or dance before;
But with ironic humour, leads us to the core:

XXII

This mystery. That in the pall of carnage,
Wispish man- like Flanders' poppies- blossoms more,
And builds with strength from stress. Thus, marriage-
Where two will rip themselves apart to shore
Up age on age what habits went afore.
Yet as the mines of Kimberley gouge deep
For diamonds, so- to glimpse the purest ore-
Must we dredge deep: through death and sleep,
Until toward that hidden power we nearer creep.

XXIII

Woman, born of woman, of woman born;
Receding in the shrouding mists of years;
Each in turn ripped from her mother; though torn,
Unchanging through all history; who tears
Has mixed with milk. What unknown future steers
Her course, repeating constant pain for love?
This aspect of their lives vain man endears,
Who hacks the flesh that women weave above;
Yet which is better loved, the vulture or the dove?

Girders in the Sand

XXIV

"**I** – who in this body; this turgent frame;
This mess of motors, pulleys, sleeves, joints, wires,
Valves and pipes; this common assemblage – came
To be. Yet could not this machine my sires
Have fabricated with turning lathes, pliers,
Drills; skilfully milled upon a steel bed
And hammered raw-red with arc-welding fires
Until, with gross movement, it's modelled head
Mimicked mine, to loll about this stage in my stead?

XXV

"**Do,** through rendition of my working parts,
Commit my body to this woman's will;
Registered eternally in nation's charts;
To use from this time forth for good or ill;
To make my mark with eager, well charged quill,
Leaving self behind." (But she, who womb-room
Leant me once for carnal knowledge to instil,
Did weave with enzyme shuttles on her loom,
Till– cast aside– she lies in sister earth's black tomb.)

XXVI

The very atoms danced their proud acclaim,
Glistening in the form they'd held unchanging
Since aeons before the world to being came-
Preformed by stellar furnace: this bright ring,
This purest elemental gold, stars bring
To being in their core – ere they explode
With primal, supernoval force to fling
Their dust across the universe. Seeds sowed
Through all of space, now fleeced from coalesced earthy lode.

XXVII

Thus Edwin put the ring upon Joy's hand,
And they were wed. His supplicating guise
(Confirmed with this expectant finger's band
Slipped gently over, to her mother's sighs,)
Was sealed with a prolonged kiss. Likewise
To all who heard was his resolved intent
Enhanced as organist did organise
More fitting music for accompaniment;
Then into Widor's Fifth, her fingers made their dent.

XXVIII

They ambled arm in arm back down the aisle,
Amongst the many faces that they knew.
Guides from Joy's young troupe lined in arching file
About the porch– a gentle wash of blue
Which Edwin and his winsome bride passed through.
To him, each guest seemed set in uniform:
As like as that confetti which folk strew;
For hat and matching coat were here the norm,
With jeans and casual jumpers counted as bad form.

XXIX

Their photographer had dashed off to the shop
For extra film; his own he'd left behind.
Returning now, he forced the pair to stop
Their natural inclination as he lined
Them once again at altar's rail, to blind
Posterity with pictures of romance,
And led them to pretend where true they'd signed;
But Joy's radiant face was no false chance:
She showed her deepest, truest love with every glance.

Girders in the Sand

XXX

Of the reception, little can I say;
The people who ate there were simple folk,
Which any age might likewise here array
With better form than these poor words evoke.
But this I'll tell: (not wishing fun to poke
At conjugal pair, whose gathering kinships
Were not theirs to assemble or revoke)
That some were present here which better lips
Might talk away and leave, tightly leashed in life's slips.

XXXI

A social worker was young cousin Phil,
Whose aged countenance betrayed his stress;
Engaged for many years on that treadmill
Of bearing up his clients in distress:
Especially those with children in a mess
From rank abuse or base deprivation–
Until one died. They didn't then Phil bless,
But slandered with vile disapprobation.
Now he takes their children without consternation.

XXXII

Uncle Henry sat alone, though Joy gave
Him her kiss. His troubled wife had laboured
One son– whose note was not of Henry's stave,
For he was then in closed prison chambered.
It's tiny neck with pink ribbon she sabred,
Then wrapped with blood-stained bundles in a bag,
Asking her own mother, whom she neighboured,
To throw them out; but she spied the pink tag.
So Henry sits alone: his wife became the lag.

XXXIII

In one corner, an aged maiden aunt
Engaged the vicar in desultory chat;
Her liveliest thought was finding time to rant
Abandonedly of the bride's mother's hat.
The vicar smiled indulgently through that,
Then turned to other women who did wait
For platitudes served without caveat.
He had lost his faith, with diminished gate;
But which was lost the first, he lacked the truth to state.

XXXIV

By strange coincidence, there chanced to be
Another of ecclesiastic haught.
The Reverend William Hunter's church was Free–
Free from all outside influence or thought,
With modern science scorned by him as naught
But 'devil's work'. These fundamental views
Of floods and starry domes, as Moses taught,
Oft led him to inflict a mental bruise
On weaker minds, whose credulity he'd well use.

XXXV

His ancestors had held the earth was flat,
And centred on that stage of mighty space
Which Ptolemy, with epicyclic bat,
Had hit upon the world. Although this trace
Of sacred, ancient lore he could displace
From modern mind, the Reverend still believed
That God moved not at evolution's pace,
But with some cosmic bang He had achieved
The fecund earth's end state... until for man He grieved!

Girders in the Sand

XXXVI

Great Aunt Olive was of this Reverend's flock:
Captivated by his eloquent tongue
So well, till of the world she took no stock
But spoke his thoughts, as each bright day was long,
And made her daughter Lisa sing this song,
That "evil is each thought we ever know!"
Until so scared she knew not right from wrong,
And each emotion was afraid to show–
With not one hope of men to make her pale cheek glow.

XXXVII

Not just her sexual urge did Lisa lose;
She could not bear to touch, or touched to be,
And pretty top or dress she'd never choose-
Lest in the mirror by her bed she'd see
Vain imagery with yearned thoughts of beauty.
Fondness for food was likewise disallowed,
Though this conflicted with her mother's plea
To eat what she was given: thus they rowed,
Till sly regurgitation let her win unbowed.

XXXVIII

Yet more than this did Lisa bravely bear
(Who hovered in that twilight entre-zone
Twixt what might be to come and present fear);
She knew death as some long unanswered 'phone
Which summoned her with oft repeated moan
To answer him. Her stripped sleeve showed the scars
Of battles borne in grief, when loud she'd groan
With stainless blade against her skin, in wars
She'd never won: her split mind matched those fleshy sores.

The Marriage of Edwin

XXXIX

The Reverend Hunter knew God's inner mind,
(For he had read a book which told of it,)
And– catching Edwin– spoke words most unkind:
That he was damned to some eternal pit–
Unless agreeing with the Reverend's Writ.
He had from now until the day he died
To change his ways, and make his life more fit;
Not just his life, but thoughts and dreams beside!
If Reverend William Hunter spoke the truth– God lied.

XL

The book of which he spoke was very old;
(Was truth increased by more antiquity?)
Much viciousness described made Edwin cold-
They seemed to thrive on vile iniquity.
Was wine from water really God's veracity?
These thaumaturgics left Edwin unbowed;
And dead men rising up was pure mendacity!
Did sperm float down from Heaven in a cloud?
Yet minds could think – this miracle Edwin allowed.

XLI

On the highest table sat a youngster:
A sullen lad of thirteen who would say
To all who'd listen, like some foolish prankster,
He'd no ken for proceedings of the day.
This youngest brother often went astray;
He seemed to wish to break up his home life
And seek amongst his friends some wilder way,
(Who shared strange smokes, while carrying a knife,)
And gave wilful distress to Edwin and his wife.

Girders in the Sand

XLII

His father long had sought this youth to tame
With disciplined reproaches, looks or word
Of chastisement, proportional to his shame.
But brother George gave no sign that he heard,
While answering with banged doors; and he sweared!
George, when firm punishment was meted out,
Retaliated by the way he lured
Social workers in when given a clout,
Who railed long at his dad, and said he was the lout.

XLIII

Joy's teacher sympathised with Edwin's dad,
While sitting at a table by the wall
Partaking of the buffet meal; she had
Heard before from Joy what might befall
The lad. Her present charges equally, though small,
Caused trouble incommensurate with their size
And acted as if each were six feet tall,
And tripped her up and spat on her with lies,
Lacking the control corporal punishment supplies.

XLIV

Aunt Norma bore chastening biology,
Her heart rotating wrongly at her birth
To yield what's called Fallot's Tetralogy,
With great vessels doing less than their full worth
Till, blocked with emboli, blood was a dearth,
And her legs and arms were amputated.
Though then eighteen, her gay infectious mirth
Did not diminish, but seemed elated
As her limbs with iron appliances were weighted.

The Marriage of Edwin

XLV

Succeeding which she crashed and lost an eye
By flying through a broken car windscreen,
But even at this loss she would not cry,
While looking for some humour she might glean
From her escape; and dark soft hair she'd preen
To show the world she still had cause to care
For her appearance; and her flat she'd clean
Though not able to climb a single stair.
She fought the world, to live more than most ever dare.

XLVI

In one dark corner, huddled, hidden faced,
There sat a friend from Edwin's earliest youth–
An artist who cared not the food to taste,
But viewed the whole assemblage as his booth
Put there for him to paint and draw each tooth
And show, Picasso-style, his inner glee.
He captured on that canvas spread, in truth,
An image of himself, with beard and bended knee,
His modesty declaimed by objectivity.

XLVII

Across the hall a lively crowd had gathered
Where jugglers and magicians entertained.
Close by these, thick perspiration lathered,
An escapologist in fetters chained
(Enough to hold the Ark back when it rained)
Defied them all to bind him– then he'd start!
He grunted, heaved and swore as pain he feigned–
Until the rigged caboodle burst apart,
With cheers to make a mere spoon-bender eat his heart.

Girders in the Sand

XLVIII

But one sad act brought pain into the day:
A lonely, simple man, none took aright,
Who called the strangest forces into play
With morphic resonance. He was not bright,
Yet claimed the whole world suffered with his blight,
With heads as empty as his own thick neep.
He held that using brains to think was trite,
For clouds sufficed his own weak thoughts to keep–
Since in his youth he had been rolled on by a sheep.

XLIX

Uncle Ted was famous for his meanness.
His great house had but one small, single room
Wherein he lived, boasting of his leanness,
Eating stale bread, and jam with mouldy bloom;
Lit by a small, bare bulb to spread the gloom.
He never showed response to caller's bell,
But sat with ancient books awaiting doom,
And wondered why his joints began to gel
Within his lonely, cold, neglected hermit cell.

L

Once, because no strangers were admitted,
He received from the Board a hefty bill
For electricity consumed: unread
On his meter – but they assumed it still,
And said, "A home so large must he well fill
With all the latest gadgets; plus heating!"
He'd always paid on time, even when ill,
And this legal demand for settling,
For forty Watts of bare light, was the final sting.

The Marriage of Edwin

LI

Without delay, contacting the Gas Board,
He took an old and brilliant gas globe lamp,
Eliciting from their showroom quite a word
To find parts fit for uncle to revamp.
Then through the ceiling-rose he soon did tamp
And linked it up: the old lead pipe still served.
The Electric Board assumed he was a scamp,
And cut him off – "It's just what he deserved!"
But from his chosen stubbornness, he'd not be swerved.

LII

He claimed the light gave softer, warmer glows
Than cold electric bulb's harsh, glaring ray;
Beside, the extra heat helped beat the snows
And saved him using candles on a tray.
The meterman turned up with police one day,
At which uncle was forced to let him in;
But on the bill, 'twas him they had to pay:
For years they'd overcharged! He had to grin,
And to Joy's wedding came to boast above the din.

LIII

These threads of typified humanity–
Through genetic sortilegeousness
Which link what's done with what is yet to be,
And coupled with environmental stress–
Formed Edwin's past and held him with duress,
Leading by force unseen, as Balaam's beast;
Traducing noble deeds as ropes enmesh.
Chained and driven to his wedding feast,
He pondered how man's greatest deeds become his least.

Girders in the Sand

LIV

He spoke and thanked all they who could attend;
Then, thanking with remembrance absent friends,
Read felicitous telegrams: "We send
Best wishes to the happy pair", which lends
Tradition to our lovers' timeless trends.
The bride next rose in contrary tradition
To give, with just piquancy, amends
For females' subjugated past position,
And thanked her groom. Applause greeted her rendition.

LV

The time at last came for them to depart
From eating what their stomachs would allow.
Joy turned and let swift, sidelong glances dart
Across the room where Edwin, like a plough,
Had gorged great furrows in the food. His brow
Took on an air of quizzicality–
And then he smiled and with the slightest bow
He took her side with assiduity–
Until they left the room with due finality.

LVI

The van he'd left he hardly recognised:
His friends had gaily decked it overall
With ribbons, tin cans, balloons and outsized
Right boots, which – aided by a loud catcall–
Accompanied the start of their long haul
Across the moors to reach their chosen town,
Where Joy at peace could now let fall
Her concentration, and her silken gown
With readiness appropriate for lying down.

The Marriage of Edwin

LVII

And lay Joy did in Edwin's arms– at peace,
With sweet contentment at his sonorous rills.
Cocooned in mighty strength within the crease
Of his curved hand, they spoke their bills,
And each from each received those sensuous thrills
Which lusty lovers reap when mutual moved
Till calm, deep, searching looks their passion stills.
Edwin gazed long – and if each glance improved
The object glanced upon in beauty, 'twas here proved.

LVIII

Her hair, in soft ambered lights, smooth as fur,
Crowned her gentle brow in rich, jewelled gold
Above laughing, green-flecked lanterns of her
Eyes; eyes which never wonders ceased behold
In every creature – sprightly, ill or old–
But saw that Heaven dwelt in those deformed,
With none on earth to whom her God was cold.
Her dextrous, practised fingers soothed and warmed
Away his worldly cares which inwardly still stormed.

LIX

He loved as in a dream, and dreamt he saw–
Where once soft clay was moulded hand on cone–
A mighty chasm opening before,
Cleft by a striking chisel splitting stone,
With inner granularity now shown.
And through this rock, upon the fertile ground,
He saw strange, hidden subtleties of tone
Which caught the flashing lights, off water bound
Within this deep carved gorge; which swelled, and grew
renowned.

Girders in the Sand

LX

Pulsating rhythms flailed the heavy air;
Cascading rocks crashed, loud upon the plain
Where that first river wandered; who could bear
To sit idly, amidst such feverish pain?
Not lords of all creation could restrain
That bursting cataclysm of deep dread,
Which welled and gushed forth like Alph's mighty main
To pour its torrents through the chasm-head,
Vanishing from view to a frozen cavern bed.

LXI

It grew dark. Whisped clouds caught the dying sun.
Muffled sounds of unwatched television
Echoed from the room below. All was done.
Joy ran a bath, measured with precision;
Edwin lay, with sweated indecision.
They wandered down to see the restaurant;
The chef spoke snootily with derision,
It was too late for Cordon vol-au-vent:
Omelettes and salads were all he had to flaunt.

LXII

Hand in hand upon the couch, the couple
Sat in secret, silent tumult. Edwin
Nestled to his bride; her hand was supple
To his touch. Knowing not where to begin,
He gave her a quick, self-effacing grin,
And asked if she had heard the news of Jane,
Whose demise augmented his guilty sin.
Joy had heard it, but said yet greater pain
Must be in they who'd driven her to dash her brain.

The Marriage of Edwin

LXIII

By his distress, the fateful die was cast;
Joy had wit to ken his full involvement.
In fitful sobs, Edwin confessed his past:
How he had loved Jane; how her will he'd bent
And then dismissed her, penniless for rent.
These searing thoughts burnt deep and made him wild;
Jane, with his pushes, was to her death sent!
Joy spoke with love and calmness – till he piled
Upon these deeds, that he was father of the child.

LXIV

Could pity change the past, it would do so–
Then in vain were all his tears and anguish.
Joy, with soft reason, tried to stem the flow–
His self recriminations abolish–
But all her art could not this accomplish.
Edwin thought by her words she did not care,
And shouted back with anger: loud, foolish,
Painful words, at which Joy could not forbear:
"Not to support the child was woefully unfair!"

LXV

Edwin screamed back– she did not understand!–
And tried to justify his past neglect,
Using those long excuses men keep canned
To ward off guilt of those sad lives they've wrecked;
But this on Joy had minimal effect.
He called her stupid then, and made inane
Remarks that she her own past should inspect–
In fact, he ranted like a man insane,
Until she could not his fierce, mad rage contain.

Girders in the Sand

LXVI

Keeping her manner and appearance mild,
Young Joy, in total innocence, asked him
Who now would make provender for the child.
Edwin acted like one who had grown dim–
As too much wine the intellect will trim–
And asked what evil was this thing she said?
And she, eyes moist about their reddened rim,
Told that the girl – his child – was not dead
But lived; for this she'd heard one hour before they'd wed.

LXVII

He paused then, and considered thus his fault:
That through the child he might make amends.
Her pregnancy had been like a shot bolt;
Discharged by parents, then disowned by friends,
She'd slipped into that limbo-land that wends
Beneath the surface of respectfulness;
Beyond where love or reason still attends.
Edwin had got her first into this mess;
Posthumous reparation might the balance redress.

LXVIII

So long he paused; then quietly he spoke,
With sorrow and regret that he had brought
Such hard agony: firstly, Jane's life he broke;
Then – from Joy's special day – he'd anguish wrought;
And now a tiny child was left with naught.
She lived – yet living knew no more than strife;
No relatives or friends who might be sought
To comfort and protect from worldly knife.
So Edwin vowed he would defend her with his life.

LXIX

Joy heard this out with inner, seething shame,
And totally refused to leave that night!
It was her wedding eve; was she to blame?
If Edwin chose to leave, that was his right–
But naught he said would drag her on that flight!
So Edwin left, alone. And Joy sat very still–
So numbed she could not cry at Edwin's slight.
She heard his van race loudly down the hill
And gulped, dry mouthed, upon life's noxious, bitter pill.

LXX

Her life had been to music given from three;
She'd held the songs of childhood in her heart
And danced through school and friendships with pure glee,
With no discord since her first cry's impart–
Till drawn to this, a target for his dart.
With solemn purpose, to her gown she crept
And ripped it through. The veil she tore apart,
Then lay upon the bed and shook and wept
Until, exhausted, with the coming dawn she slept.

The Tale of Mary-Anne

He paced the days with lonely, anxious tread,
Broken by fitful interludes of sleep.
She, by his patient hand alone, was fed:
No other came; none wished the child to keep,
Until that time he was allowed to leave
And take her home, on hearing from the court.
He loved her dearly, and helped her to grieve
Their common loss; paternity he sought,
While flinging public scandals to the wind.
(He had no contact with his wife; but friends
Said she'd left the town. He would not rescind
His step by one toe's length which such harm mends.)

And thus she grew – and growing, made him yearn
For knowledge wide, whose lack drove him to learn.

* * * * *

Edwin discovers a fresh leaf
From bitter fruit born in grief,
 And turns it in his hand.
And all man's knowledge seeks to find
When a child's wondering mind
 Asks how the world was planned.

The Tale of Mary-Anne

Eight candles burnt: the pink-iced cake
Glowed fluorescent from the flickering light;
A web of fine, white tracery
Declared the feast of Mary-Anne;
With trifles, sausages and buns
Devoured with dedication.
No unease or hesitation
Spoilt these children's simple fun;
They sang their songs and joined her games,
Until the last one was reclaimed
By its mother from the feasting,
And Edwin's parents bade farewell.
Then Mary-Anne delightedly
Ran up the stairs to newest toys.
Her dark, long hair and distant looks,
Her secret ways and solemn thoughts,
With sudden smiles and bursts of song
Endeared her to him deeply:
Now sang she ancient lullabies–
While Edwin sat alone.

He'd cared for her for five full years,
Through nursery and school.
He'd paid a woman across the street
To fill those hours he could not meet–
But less so now than hitherto.
Quick-pulsed, he'd nursed her through ill health,
And seen her artwork at the school;
Taken her on special trips;
Met her from her own friends homes;
And– all to tell– had been to her
A father, friend and councillor,
Squeezing from both ends of work his time.

Girders in the Sand

This was the gall– his erstwhile job:
Demanding all for profits' sake,
Unbending in its selfish creed,
Insisting that he gave his all–
But he had not. And with the fall
Of profits came his shoddy end.
They spied on him and found he was not there:
And blamed on him such seldom missing shoe
As might occur from time to time
In any firm; but from this leverage
They'd prised him out– and sacked him.
So now he sat alone and pondered:
What the future might contain;
How best he might now qualify,
Or for some other task retrain.
Above the room he heard her laugh,
The song of carefree Mary-Anne,
And smiled within– glad now that he
Could for himself life freely span
And care for her more properly:
Being home to her call,
Or walking weekends through the park.
Yet fresh small clouds formed over all:
For the car he'd have to sell;
And curtail their holiday.
He resolved to speak of it–
But not today, her special day!

A Day At The Seaside

The sea-god is the sea, and the sea stays our god still;
And we carry the sea within us:
Dank demesne of the surgent tide
That breaks our time in a rhythm of dreams
To cast us up on the day-dead beach.
Lowering skies subsume our forms, and wait—
Till time-engendered, sorbile drops
Stir new forms, to imitate a deity.

* * * * *

With the forming of the seasons,
He had fallen yet more slothful;
All her favourite, awkward questions
He had further tried to stifle:

"Why do stars shine in the dark
        And who first switched them on?
"Why's the sky a sparkling blue—
        And where has mummy gone?
"Why is sea wet on the sand,
        And how long is the shore?
"Why can I see through a glass
        But not a wooden door?
"What is it that's really me?
        What am I made for?"

Until, exasperated by them,
And to prove he was a man,
He set out to seek some answers,
Both to seem less ignorant—
And that a child might know better,

37

Girders in the Sand

That in her eyes he might broaden
As he gained and grew in knowledge.
This too fitted with his promise
At the Centre for Employment
That he'd seek another job soon,
Or obtain some higher grading;
Studies to improve his standing
With employers: 'twas the rage.
So, without a second's glancing
At alternatives in hand,
He rushed and joined a night school course in
Natural Science. It sounded grand.

* * * * *

She had a strange, compelling visage
With the darkest hidden eyes,
Which cut into his mind like rapiers,
Slicing up his hidden, dark thoughts
Showing them as something fresher.
Then with certainty he knew it;
Yes, he knew with convert's passion
That he must divest all nature
Of her secrets, and her meanings,
Till he saw her hidden patterns
With the same dissected pieces
As she saw his concealed yearnings:
This dark tutor from the college,
With her mocking taunts and laughter,
And half-hidden implications
That his best thoughts were as nothing.

He would prove he was her equal–
Fit to match her in all learning,
Fit to take some place of honour

A Day At The Seaside

In this new world of the scholar;
In this world where 'why?' is wise.

* * * * *

All the constraints of the heavens,
All the mysteries of the salt seas,
All the memories of the deep rocks,
Swept into his gaze with ease.
His tutor at the night school leant him
A vidarium to use at home;
Hooked into his television,
He'd no need libraries to roam:
Just the dials he had to twiddle
To bring in view all data known.
Set the year, or place, or person,
And the screen– with life its own–
Would summon up all that it could:
Pixeled action on a stage–
Based on drawings, prints or art–
Would move with motions recognised,
Speaking words put in its heart
From all archives of world renown;
Reading, speaking, with the sound
Of authenticity.
Another dial, and he could probe
The depths of space,
Or swiftly race
Into the atom's core.

And what was more,
The formulae of what was known
Were there presented, simply
or with contiguous confusion,
As might his need demand.

Girders in the Sand

So at his own pace he could go,
Surveying those fine depths below
The limits of eyed resolution.
O, it was a fine machine–
And anything still left unseen
He could approach his tutor with,
And she would guide him through it all:
She of the emerald home-spun tabard,
Flecked throughout with primrose hues.

Thus did Edwin start his task–
Cheryl would direct his path
From time to time;
But text books were there none;
It now was up to him.

* * * * *

In a corner, by the window,
On a table, plugged in ready,
Sat the silent gift of science.
Edwin closed the door most softly,
Slightly nervous of its power–
That a box so small and compact
Could contain more than his brain,
And reveal all nature's secrets
Culled by noble men of learning
Giving lifetimes of devotion
To the cause of furthering knowledge.
So, with cautious apprehension,
He switched on the vidarium,
Well resolved to learn his lesson,
Seeking how life had begun.

The Beagle

First Fruits

What moves a man to forfeit life– though small–
Upon the roll of one capricious dice?
Security and pleasure were his call;
    Why then did death or danger him entice?
If ever reasons bloomed to linger yet
Before a happy hearth of love and care,
Such reasons Darwin had already met:
Yet sensuous lust could not his mind ensnare.
With eager breath, fate took him on its wing
Till, soaring like a liberated eagle,
The rain-swept decks and rigging seemed to sing–
Sweeping him along to man the Beagle.

No grand achievements wait on man's desire–
Who'll rest content to sit before sloth's fire.

* * * * *

    Now Edwin sees that death rules all,
    Forcing change through bloody pall,
      To guide what will survive:
    Perfection wrought on forge of hell.
    Bound forever by time's spell,
      New creatures rise, alive.

The Beagle

Charles Darwin (1809–1882)
Captain Robert FitzRoy (1805–1865)

Walled with an image of greenery round him,
  Stretching from carpet to plastered cornice;
Filling the room of his mind with its pictures:
  Sounds from the chaffinch to snake's lowly hiss.

All life's diversity spread wide before him,
  Flashed on his screen in its caricatured way;
Dolphins leapt, adders slid, corncrakes gavotted;
  Plants in gross raiment now coloured his day.

Kites brightly spiralling over the roof tops;
  Whiskered mice sniffing the ripe ears of corn;
Toothed beavers building and tortoises hatching;
  Cats on wide prairies were eyeing the dawn;

Confusions of butterflies curtained the summer;
  Stotting gazelles jumped to startle the air;
Gibbering monkeys cartwheeled in the forest;
  Brown, fluffy cubs stalked a lone, silent bear.

Over the great sea and through the wide ocean
  Swarming with living things both great and small,
There played Leviathan in the blue waters:
  Molluscs and fishes were there to enthral.

Blackbirds with head turned awaited the earthworm;
  Bats with their sonar ears gimballed with glee;
Bees oozed their honey and danced for its making;
  Life teamed in each little niche he could see.

The Beagle

Curved for its prey was the beak of the eagle,
　Talons and pinions spread wide in decent;
Wheeling birds soared; the wild shriek of a seagull
　Summoned diversity's clear argument.

　　　　　* * * * *

Courtly, unbending, and aristocratic,
　Born to the sea yet the son of an Earl,
Captain FitzRoy held command of the Beagle–
　Absolute, resolute, fixed by his will:

Five years to fathom the seas and the coastlines,
　Charting far ports where the bold Jack unfurled.
Firmly, FitzRoy chose the crew for his vessel–
　Gathered in Plymouth to girdle the world:

Sailmaker, carpenter, mates and lieutenants;
　Swarthy young riggers, artist, and boatswain;
Surgeon and cook; midshipmen and surveyor;
　Tried volunteers for the heaving ocean.

Captain FitzRoy held deep-rooted convictions,
　Acting with firm faith in all that he did;
Just one man more was required for the Beagle:
　Called to discover what nature had hid.

　　　　　* * * * *

Darwin, a sportsman in vivid red tunic,
　Clattering the cobbles of Christ's College court,
Handed his gun to a groom with his charger
　After a good morning's hunting and sport.

Girders in the Sand

Utter delight broke across his fresh features:
  After uncertainty came his degree.
He'd nearly drowned in mathematical symbols,
  Hated the classics and loathed liturgy.

Only his collecting aroused him to passion:
  Even his mouth he would store beetles in
Given the urgency of some fresh species,
  Yet with his mouth full he managed to grin,

Until its foul, acrid, pungent secretions
  Forced him to spit it away in disgust,
Leaving him loathing himself for his weakness–
  Next time on collecting-tins he'd better trust.

"Combine your passions – be a soft country clergyman,"
  Cautioned his father while sitting at ease.
"Surely your cousin will tempt you to listen?
  It's safe and respectable – and her you will please."

* * * * *

"God is my reference in all my endeavours;
  Your part is vital," the Captain declared.
"Find me fresh proof of the truth of the bible.
  To this fine calling we'll both be well paired.

"Share half my cabin and dine at my table–
  I value your work as a necessity.
Some fools have doubted the facts of creation!"
  Darwin agreed to each point willingly;

The Beagle

Brave words, resounding through centuries of schism,
  Filling believers with mistrust and dread.
Captain FitzRoy helped him sort out his hammock:
  A leader of men – yet refined and well bred.

Soft ticking clocks break the time into minutes;
  Twenty or more were displayed on his shelf,
Setting the limits of earth as they circled:
  Each measured longitude limits himself.

The day they departed was like a great birthday:
  December, the twenty-seventh day, they slipped berth,
Through grey gales lashing the seas into mountains;
  Mal de mer ailed him – to the crew's gentle mirth!

Hawsers were hauled to the fife's steady rhythm;
  Summoned by Coxswain's pipe, boys raced aloft,
Shaking the sails from the yards and fixed rigging;
  Tuned to the sea as they crested and troughed.

Ten mounted guns leant grim hope to survival;
  Oaken beams creaked under smooth teaked top decks;
Twin masts of pine caught the power of the gallants:
  Rolling, the brig drew abaft the buoyed wrecks.

Dark stained mahogany lining the cabins
  Shuddered like tense cats awaiting each wave.
Overhead hammering pounded the caulking,
  Keeping seams watertight 'gainst Neptune's grave.

Crossing the line in traditional manner,
  Turning the hands up and shortening the sail,
Pitch, paint and lather recruited the griffins;
  Even the Captain was wet by their pail.

Girders in the Sand

Landfall was made amidst darkening verdure,
   Towering loftily mile after mile.
FitzRoy stayed head to the wind for the evening,
   Entering Rio next morning in style.

One of the fishermen hooked a diodon,
   Incarnadining the seas in its rage;
Puffed to a globular, evil distension,
   Toughened sharks' bellies cannot this encage.

Seeing a wasp and large spider do battle
   Showed with fatality skirmishes waste;
Searching then lancing its victim's abdomen
   Till, mortally wounded, by poisons effaced.

Silently marching through tracks in the jungle,
   Ever advancing, ne'er to retreat,
Circling round helpless lizards in panic,
   Myriads of army ants kill all they meet.

More vicious still was the martinet slaver:
   Whipping, belittling and branding by spite;
Arbitrary hanging, or maiming, or prison,
   Rendered these abject men less than one mite.

"Slaves are essential to run the plantations,"
   With patient solemnity FitzRoy averred.
"Nothing is said in the bible against them!"
   Darwin reacted with contempt and sneered.

Megalith bones littered cliffs Patagonian–
   Vast, countless species now lying extinct.
Darwin proposed they had once ruled this region;
   FitzRoy's reply was forthright and succinct.

The Beagle

Craggy rocks, bound in their minds from first childhood,
  Solidly fashioned, eternity fake:
Suddenly– cracking like shells to a knife thrust–
  Buildings and men fell with fearful earthquake.

Fuegian cannibals roasted their mothers;
  One cracked a boy's skull for dropping sea-eggs.
Yet three same savages, though hardly human,
  By FitzRoy's bounty had grown Christian legs.

FitzRoy had held Captain Cook as his hero,
  Giving his life to the utmost extent.
Fighting the Horn through a newly found channel
  Named for the Beagle, hell's curtains were rent.

One peak was named in high honour of Darwin:
  Threatening to leave them cut off and afloat,
Slabs of blue ice fell and threw high seas over them;
  Darwin's quick bravery saved them their boat.

Captain FitzRoy steered the skiff to an atoll;
  Darwin took soundings with tallowed lead line:
Finding the coral rose sheer in the ocean
  Showed them the bottom had sunk in the brine.

On finches he focused, in varied profusion:
  Each on its island allotted one place.
Darwin envisaged them drift on the currents;
  Now interbreeding, each bred a new race.

Clutches of eggs hatched each year to each mother:
  Surely their numbers should show no restraint?
Foes and starvation soon ripped and devoured them:
  Eternal slaughter's knife made him feel faint.

Girders in the Sand

Tortoises toppling over the cliff face
  Showed how untimely to life they were patched;
So many fresh ones were laid– yet each season
  Buzzards were filching their young as they hatched.

* * * * *

On his return to the green Wolds of England,
  Darwin reflected on all he had seen;
Millions of years beyond mind to ring changes,
  Forming the present. With resolute mien,

Finally wrote he contentious conclusions,
  Based on firm knowledge of nature's own laws:
That life, appearing in all its abundance,
  Rose from the simplest of primitive spores.

Huxley and Wilberforce argued at Oxford
  Over the merits of Darwin's ideas.
Captain FitzRoy waved his bible above him
  And cried with impassioned faith, hiding his fears,

"My life was lived for the pursuit of knowledge,
  Pushing the curtains of evil away.
Here I have read you my text on storm theory;
  Now greater storms than at sea will hold sway.

"This man is worse than the Fuegian savage
  (Whose ignorance is his own self defence);
Each time I aided him, counselled, assisted,
  This damned sciolist was plotting nonsense."

The Beagle

FitzRoy wheeled round like an avenging prophet,
   Haughty, aloof, with contemptuous pride,
Stormed from the hall in his unbending fury
   Until he broke: by his own hand he died.

Red were the gaunt hands that wielded the death blow;
   Crimson the last words that welled from the teeth.
Staining the greenery, blooding the carpet,
   Robert FitzRoy had just death to bequeath.

* * * * *

Breathless, Edwin paused and pondered.
All the dark dreams of creation,
All the terror of man's being,
Brought in thought to one sapient:
Death was all that guided living.
Man was but an outgrown monkey,
Fighting to sustain more fighting,
In the body chance provided;
Even mind was one more tissue:
Outpouching of neocortex
Carrying his noble yearning
From a simpler archecortex
With no hope of ever winning.
He raced out to contact Cheryl,
Rushed to seek balm for disquiet,
Frenzied hoping that his substance
Might be more than blind chance only.

Cheryl led him to a valley
Hidden in a sunny daleside,
Where the water gushed and founted
Over blocks of limestone terrain,
Sparkling in the autumn sunset;

Girders in the Sand

And he hid behind the torrents,
Splashed by cooling back-blown cascades,
Watching trout that leaped about him
While the rabbits lopped beside them,
And the birds played in the brambles
Which bent low to kiss the water.
Then she smiled and touched him softly–
Saying he was part of nature.
Evolution may move blindly,
But it moved for ever onward,
Building out of all proceeding.
Nothing dropped on earth from heaven;
Nothing need disturb his balance;
For he knew his simple substance
Was the sum of living millions
Who'd moved through the world before him,
Growing slowly in their structure;
Building surely, ever growing,
In complexity and detail,
Growing steadily from features
Left upon the earth at birth.
Then she showed how all were brothers;
How to each was each allied;
Man to mammal; bird to earthworm;
Toad to virus. Though each died,
Yet the thread of life within them
Lived for ever. Edwin sighed,
And calmed by this, he promised then
Feverishly to study more–
To seek that thread which linked his core.

* * * * *

The Beagle

She laughed, and her laughter echoed the dark hollows
Of our long-dead men;
tubes of time, sucking up all past potential,
spewing out a dismal future:
tunnels of dry nothing, leading nowhere–
but the inky blankness of never-seen infinity.
Bewildering confabulations pressed on an eerie present
like the onus of dead eagles,
weighing our great guilt, and bowing our bruised heads,
in low subjugation
to her full derision
of heroic man's pretence.

The Nobel Pilgrimage

Alfred Bernhard Nobel (1833–1896)

Unprepossessing, gawky, unmarked birth
Were in his clay compounded. Slack he'd been
To learn at school; a lad of no great worth;
But sad, long looks and vacant, pallid mien
Hid no base, subtle cravings in his smile.
Yet though uncurious his form to know,
His languid, distant poise betrayed no guile.
Young Nobel was his name, and worthy so;
Though oft his parents did him roughly chide
For feelings of unpatronymic shame,
And urged him take true, welcome, fervent pride–
Who could not languish with more modest name.

The noble deeds he willed through death were vast:
To dynamite achievements by his blast.

* * * * *

With chemistry life first began,
From primeval soup to man,
    With smooth evolving thread.
Each succeeding generation
Through new specialisation,
    Its common source will shed.

The Nobel Pilgrimage

The Monk

Gregor Mendel (1822–1884)

Dark, high, shadowed columns filled the screen
when, to his ears, came sombre organ tones,
dissolving in monastic, ghostly sheen
to mingle with the monks' lamenting groans.
Janacek, in playing music mighty,
measured rhythmically these people's needs;
sanctified a gentle abbot's piety
on organ pipes and resonating reeds.

(Within the coffin Edwin tried to peer:
so dark! Things moved at his unpractised hand
too fast; he turned the dial back year by year;
the abbot shot up, raced back through the land,
then stopped: he was a simple farmer's son.
More slowly, Edwin traced where he'd begun.)

Old feudal laws held Anton Mendel bound
to work his liege-lord's lands three days in six;
his only heir and son, with genius crowned,
still had to tend the flocks and mend hayricks.
This quiet, modest, stubborn farmer's boy,
named Gregor Mendel, would dutifully employ
himself to rear his father's breeding stocks.
His intellectual gifts bred rudest shocks;
they had no money to support his need
of learning – but this potent, restless seed
had taken root within his pale, smooth brow
and – germinating there – he'd not eschew
his desperate, burning ache to learn yet more.
His father, following the feudal law,
was injured, felling in his landlord's trees.

Girders in the Sand

Gregor, refusing simple filial duties,
kept to his dream; nor would cant dignify
but sacrificed the farm to satisfy
his own desire to wrest with truth by storm,
and forewent other pleasures, taking monk's black form:
for through monastic habit he could learn,
while basic bread and clothing he would earn.

The Agricultural Society
had been transformed in Brno by Andre,
who stated, "To ensure prosperity,
agriculture must– like Newton's gravity–
discover Nature's laws, and benefit
from this fresh light which physics has now lit.
We must in duty lay down true foundations,
benefiting unborn generations,
though nothing knowing of what may be found:
except mankind may reach some higher ground."

Here many minds to strange ideas were bent;
Pasteur had yet to show how wines ferment,
and many thought the sun bred crocodiles
from the mud of river banks; or piles
of soiled, stained linen fathered baby mice,
And flies grew fresh from meat that was not 'nice'.
Theories of spontaneous creation
fitted God's divinest intervention:
who else would maggots place in rosy apples,
but He who confined men in stone-walled chapels?
But Mendel, gentle son of earth, said "No!
Like comes from like," and held this to be so:
showing in his monastery garden,
for generation after generation,
peas from parent stock bred true: short or tall
gave tall or short– not blended between all.

The Nobel Pilgrimage

And though one special characteristic
might be recessive, smothered by some trick,
it soon reverted given half a chance–
hidden, but not lost from Mendel's glance.

Thus peas become the model for the man,
each character now carried by a gene;
for this was shown from Mendel's simple plan–
and nothing else was found hid in between.
There was no vital life force. Chemistry
accounted for the *pisum's* sweet offspring
(which you and I know as the humble pea);
now chemists for one century took wing:
somewhere within each cell there is a code
that links what's gone with what is yet to be.
Just where and how life perpetrates its ode,
determination drove Edwin to see.

* * * * *

Friedrich Miescher

(1844–1895)

Herr Miescher sat despondent in the hall,
feasting with smart students of Basel
who celebrated this, their passing out,
with revelry and songs which he ought shout
loud like the rest– had not early deafness
robbed both voice and Hippocratic deftness.
The noises of the party mocked his ears
and reawakened dormant, childhood fears
in one who cherished serving through medicine–
as too his father and uncle had done.
(He once had longed to be a simple priest–

Girders in the Sand

but that was barred until his yearning ceased.)
He sat morosely, despite high status,
and watched divide the heavy curtained wall;
two matched teams of well-drilled, napkined waiters
marched down the steps to fan across the hall,
each carrying a candle in one hand.
A vintage cork-drawn Hock was served as wine;
they marched by stepping to the local band,
filled glasses, then retreated, still in line.

"Schnapps is the drink for me,
Flowing strong and flowing free,
Warming through so gently,
　　　Bring more Schnapps!

"Schnapps has a glowing tone–
It's unique, it's on its own.
With my glass I'm not alone:
　　　Bring more Schnapps!

"We love its fine bouquet,
But we'd drink it anyway–
So we sing till close of day:
　　　Bring more Schnapps!

"On the Rhine with our women:
Bisqued, flavoured pink salmon,
Served with sauces and lemon!
　　　Bring more Schnapps!

The Nobel Pilgrimage

"There is nothing we can't do,
We're noble students loud and true,
Raise your glasses to this brew–
Bring more Schnapps!

"Basel maids are so fine,
As are maidens from the Rhine;
We like beer and we like wine–
But bring more Schnapps!"

Higher they sang, till standing on the plates;
trampled food and wine mingled, flung in grates.
The loud banging of the heavy glasses
and ill-distorted, raucous, drunken voices
persuaded this young student to change tack:
on medicine finally he turned his back.

His uncle Wilhelm wrote encouragement:

"Dear Fritz,
        I cannot doubt your aptitude
for work, and I'm certain your achievement
will be high, if your optimistic mood
is well maintained. Your own self confidence
and dedication are all you require;
not empty, foolish, over-confidence
that cannot make mistakes– but to aspire
to self-reliant, continuous work:
giving of your best, you will become the best.
Though doubts in other fields will still lurk,
your individuality from the rest
will be assured; so take from this good heart
and choose your field– then set yourself apart."

Girders in the Sand

Miescher took up physiology:
the cell nucleus he chose to study,
and for a source of rounded nuclei
he thought that human lymph cells he might try;
for fetid wounds discharged too commonly.
Bacteria on instruments swarmed free,
as antisepsis was not yet founded
by Lister– thus foul, sordid wounds abounded
where the surgeon's dirty knife had been;
and copious, oozing sores could oft be seen.
Putrid bandages Miescher collected:
washing out the cells he had selected,
he studied them and took their nuclei
apart. In acid phosphorus they were high,
so Miescher named this nucleic acid.
A sugar and four bases closed the lid
on all of interest in the nucleus–
such simple chemicals were not of use
in formulating life its myriad form:
but proteins in profusion seemed to swarm
with variations in their type and length,
which many chemists took to be life's strength.

The Rockefeller Institute for Medical Research

B ricks not white, nor red, nor yellow– nondescript;
In profile low, plain, austere– and functional.
Simple form, consistent with plain purpose.
Bare efficiency, dedicated to enquiry:
Institute and man.
With blurred distinction, someone moved within;
Clothing impeccable but subdued;
Manner shy yet courteous;
Ochred with home-rolled smokes.
The Institute was set by Rockefeller;
Who set Oswald Avery?
Unique provision for laboratories was laid;
Space and equipment far excelled all needs
For simple tests.
And the man?
Mind, in excess of simple needs,
Reached through forbidding darkness.

* * * * *

Girders in the Sand

Oswald Avery

(1877–1955)

He passed through time so quickly; he was already old,
  With more years yet to tread to end the patient work.
  His jutting brow was veined; his pate had now grown bald;
The man moved slowly, seeking always where could lurk
  That one swift cause of death– searching for some hidden
mode.
  From patients, though a doctor, he now tried to shirk:
Bacteriology was his dedicated code
  For helping heal the sick. By him, pneumonia
  Was cultured in two forms: one small which smoothly flowed,
Yet killed so many it was viewed with chilling fear;
  The other, seeming roughly contoured to the eye,
  Would watch its virulence *in vivo* disappear
By painstaking dilutions. "Tell me how and why,"
  Pondered Avery with calm deliberation,
  "When given this harmless strain, healthy mice will die
From killed smooth cells in minute concentration?"
  Long, timeless days to sit or pace, and think or talk,
  With painful anxiousness for what direction,
From all those many byways down which he might walk,
  Would lead to gallant answers to this worthy quest.
  Long days in silence passed; then, like a plunging hawk,
He'd drop upon some reasoned method for the test;
  For thinking in itself is never just an end:
  Its value lies in what the well-trained mind can wrest
From keenest observations, which alone defend
  The mind from foolishness of unpricked, bubbling thought.
  He kept his lab uncluttered, without trace or blend
Of homeliness: no pictures, relics, trash nor wart
  That might reveal some common human quality.
  His bench lay bare, with plain test tubes in rows which caught
The Bunsen light, reflecting his humility.

The Nobel Pilgrimage

"The best planned methods all demand the simplest probe;
  Experimental clutter breeds banality!"
With rigorous, honed intensity, his microbe
  Grew, cultured with a solitary obsession.
  He stayed behind at night, a scientific Job,
Dedicated, gleaning facts by sharp selection.
  He boiled huge vats of beef hearts at blood heat for broth,
  Centrifuging them ice-cold with a fast motion,
Washed and cooked in brine three times to form a froth,
  Then, shaken well with bile to break the cell walls down,
  Reprecipitated by an alcoholic trough;
Digestive enzymes cleared away their sugary gown,
  And plain chloroform removed each trace of protein.
  The final fibrous strand brought Avery his crown:
It was the purest DNA, which shone so clean;
  His many years of struggle proved its purity;
  Its transformation through the death of mice was seen,
But many doubted its intrinsic verity.
  Though Avery found no protein in the slightest trace,
  Prejudiced adherents maintained their enmity,
Denying him this hard-won, vital, central ace.
  Though many times he'd struggled as he sought the way–
  Carrying his candle in this remote, darkened place–
In falling, he'd pick up a new-found piece of clay
  And fashion it to form some worth-while novel thought.
  This man, unaided, showed that simple DNA
Contains the sum of all that life has ever wrought,
  Then died. "With greater honour would our wide world sway
  Had it honoured him, and its Nobel trinkets brought,"
Spoke Chargaff, now ablaze with this inspiring ray.

Girders in the Sand

Dr Rosalind Franklin

(1920–1958)

Above the towering slabs of dolomite, the stars
  Appeared and threw the mountain folds to solid black
  Which matched in dullness all her Paris coals and chars.
Some while before, just as Earth's sun had lit each track,
  Her X-ray sun had teased those crystal structures out
  And opened nature's secret enclaves one more crack;
Now Rosalind resolved more secrets yet to rout.
  She loved to climb these hills, and measured each slight edge
  For firmness; then, well roped, she'd tackle nab or snout
And climb with certain feet and reach the top-most ledge
  To see the shadow of her frame flung far below.
  Her pocket held a letter– a driving paper wedge–
Fermenting in her mind as yeast in rising dough
  And tempting Rosalind to leave her Paris home.
  Her climbing and her memories made her young face glow
With pleasure at the feat she had achieved. A tome
  Of learned papers had built her reputation;
  She'd fought without diplomacy's false honey-comb,
Giving her a naive love of confrontation:
  Fighting with defiance her father's prejudice,
  Making science her purpose with determination
By doing one thing well; eschewing that fools' office,
  Marriage; her child must be the truth she would expose.
  She'd cycled through blitz air-raids with no cowardice,
While facing high-incendiaries among the streets and rows
  Of London homes, supporting Jewish refugees.
  Returning now, with fluent French and stylish clothes,
Devoting all her gifts to find the golden keys
  Which might unlock the very structure of the gene,
  She left for London; and began to work with ease,
Building a camera to display with marvellous mien
  The drawn-out fibres of pure DNA. One thought

The Nobel Pilgrimage

Became her task and purpose: to explore what none had
seen.
Then she, who with Meccano had simple models wrought,
  Disdaining dolls, created now a new design,
    Controlling X-ray beams with her rare skill, now brought
To focus on one form of life she could confine.
  About this time in Cambridge by strange coincidence
    Chance drew two men together as though by design
And they too asked themselves how nature might condense
  A thousand varied life forms to a common thread.
    They lacked data themselves, so looked o'er Franklin's fence
To build a trivet which to her design was wed.
  Scorning their nugatory efforts as a blight,
    She left to take more pictures that would fill her head
With wonder as each new emergent shape took flight.
  She sat before her dappled films so silently–
    Like one in temple prayer, wearing a robe of white;
True science held for her a mystic vibrancy:
  She worshipped truth and felt her pictures ought to speak,
    Contemptuously dismissing those who'd disagree
As over anxious Zealots whose minds were somewhat weak.
  Chargaff– now Avery's acolyte– had found how bases paired
    And bore his votive knowledge to the Cambridge clique,
Sarcastically deriding these two men who dared
  Upon the backs of others race to heady fame.
    Dare I relate, propitious fate let more yet be shared?
For Pauling's son next sought their room, and with him came
  News of his famous father's tries on DNA,
    Which spurred this tireless pair to try and match his game.
In London, Rosalind turned to her films to pray,
  Exposing for long hours to radiation her physique
    (Encumbrances like leaden aprons she thought fey);
Then slowly brought to light more plates with such technique,
  She fired the best shots seen across the waiting world,
    Plotting atoms' places with precision so unique

Girders in the Sand

The very strands of life were to her call unfurled.
  But unbeknown to Rosalind, two turned to look
  Who, like fresh converts to new faith, soon whirled,
Illumined by a lambent nun's inspiring book.
  Then yet again that power, which drives celerity,
  Sent one last link to forge the chain which our world shook:
One vital man who had that rare sagacity,
  Divining tautomeric shapes for every base;
  He shared their room until, with true audacity,
The puzzle's parts now fell into their final place.
  Their model has transformed our view of all we are;
  Dividing endlessly since life began its race,
And driving evolution from those shifts which mar
  The order of the bases by chance mutations:
  Increased complexity through vast millennia,
Till those subtle strands were formed whose designations
  Were Watson and his soul mate Crick, whose names adorn
  The double helix. Thus by their chance nutations,
They took that pilgrimage which brought a winter's dawn
  On Stockholm soil, to greet the gentle Swedish king
  And claim a Nobel honour for new knowledge born.
Humility and self-effacement never bring
  Mankind to bridge new chasms on the endless plain;
  Boldness to step along an unlit way and string
The labyrinth for meeker men to jump the slain
  Should earn its just reward. But strange indeed the thought
  That she who held a lamp to light the paths they gain
Then died of hidden cancer, from her own lamp caught.
  The same low sun now glinted red on Cambridge snow,
  Where generations found great truths like wires stretched taut,
Till heaven's beacons shone through silent air below
  And slipped past darkened windows of the seminars
  To set their model sparkling with a ghostly glow–
Built like a spiral stairway to the calling stars.

The Nobel Pilgrimage

Θ - ε - ρ - ω - σ
I - B - U
Do - up - we - go
They - are - bad - for
Time - gave - fear - some
Great - waste - lives - rough
Single - change - height - forced
Winter's - bleaked - feature - through.

One simple alphabet dictating life
Emergent form from complex chaos builds;
Selective repetition is its key,
Its characters, clear written here from ACT to G,
Bring blueprint for potential.
Sequenced DNA on genes:
An alphabet whose words loom infinite
In genosphere's extent,
Yielding man. Yet stay–
Save thought, this is not man!
This code for making flesh in which we dance our lives,
While lacking thought, is but the empty shell of man.
No being is foretold in bases crude,
For life comes larger than its simple code
As books surpass their pulp and ink
By content meaningful:
Provocative, or power-filled for urgency,
Or inspirational with strength to make men laugh;
While drably commonplace contain
Uniqueness in the telling of their lives.

Though every chain be to us known within the gene,
We could not guess one single arm nor eye–
Beyond our power emergent complex systems lie,
Nor any mathematics to predict.
But Cheryl chatted on awhile, and said

Girders in the Sand

If all were known at any stage it could be done;
It's ignorance that blinds us to this realm:
Prediction is but calculus writ large.

All this young Edwin could not contradict,
But vowed to drink yet deeper from Minerva's well
And chase the rays of heaven for the Grail of Truth–
That secret code, remote in time and space
Wherein lies hid the infinite abyss,
The core of man and all material stuff,
So with his mentor signed another year.

The Spring of Thought

Clouds, shaped by idle minds, slipped coolly past
While on the ocean's swelling breast, a barque
Gained bearing from the slewing winds' coarse blast
To fetch a Punic coast, with war its mark.

Set here young, fabled, jewel-decked Helen's mirth,
Lifting love to legend, from crude murder,
Watched willows' trailing brushes stroke her earth,
Shaded by translucent, dappled verdure.

Long Trojan wars' brave battles and swift kill
Left builded City States which still may thrall,
Moved men to music, by a dream-like skill–
Till cropped with lava as a tumbling wall.

Here, on these Isles of Greece where gods once stirred,
The harpist's muted strings are softly heard.

* * * * *

Young Edwin in his second year
Studies what the Greeks held dear:
  Purest astronomy.
But much meandering slows his path,
Risking Cheryl's scathing wrath,
  Lured by astrology.

Girders in the Sand

First Breath

I

Of that lost moment when our kind fresh moved, ill-torn
From failing forest, cursed to hunt with stealth and wit
Upon fertile Savannah plains; when consciousness
Through emptiness first seeped and stirred primeval man
From bare-breathed existence, to pause and upward glance,
To catch the seasons strewn across the belt of heaven.
Edwin peered back through mists of greedy time to search
That unctuous age, with seeded thoughts now pregnant
made,
By intense reverence bred of revelations new;
He saw a daily fire cross a vaulted sky
Vast times before his bridled fires were taboo welt,
Then, falling like a subject lord, grace-filled he knelt.

II

Out-pouring virgin praise for regularity,
To mark the years in that new garden, stones were set:
Slabbed monoliths fine-hewn and dragged by stubborn
men
To build a henge or pyramid and scar their earth
With high honour for the divine lights of heaven.
Prolific tribes fixed seasons from the orbing marks,
With repetitious Zodiacal starry signs;
Or else compiled by radiant moon's soft ebb and flow
Their priestly calendars for crop and harvest time;
Some turned the astral symbols for their artful guile
Acclaiming of themselves rules others laboured for–
With forecast, swelling grain replenishing their store.

The Spring Of Thought

III

And all this time as crops swelled plump, and wars were
fought;
While children cried and horses tamed to steer a plough;
With fires kept and cooking done about crude hearths
Not knowing if their solemn labours might yield fruit
In times yet unimagined to their rustic days,
Some few lone men tracked and marked their observations.
Great Empires feed on calendars for rote and tithe;
First with precision Babylonians captured time
And caged it, extruding years by seconds counted,
With stark eclipses noted well and marvelled at,
To keep the fleeting instant for generations,
Until their torch passed on, down succeeding nations.

IV

Though no one man could dare compute the course of
heaven,
Yet some there were who puzzled at the wayward signs:
Slight noted shifts within the ordered span of lights;
While agile planet wanderers would errant run,
Charted by watchful men through scores of centuries.
Egyptian goddess Isis named bright Sirius,
Whose dawn approach foretold the rising, fertile Nile:
Yet even she would lag two weeks each thousand years,
Until too tardy to predict a flooding land.
This long, through dynasties of Pharaohs, did it take
To chart numerous regressions in the mystic seven,
And note a perturbation in the spin of heaven.

Girders in the Sand

V

Now bloody war, allied to self-interested states,
Becomes the backdrop to an envied, thrusting age,
Natal by degree to visionary men
Who mark the spheres of heaven with geometry:
Dividing lands by straight-edged rule and compasses
To straddle continents and touch the distant stars.
They lay a measure to the ceaseless, strutting moon,
Computing breadth and height above this fractious earth
From records past of lonely men. These gods of Greece
Who leave convention's haven far beneath contempt,
Do dare ascend the awesome slopes of ignorance,
Generating concepts, like true monarchs, by their stance.

VI

Edwin's swift stare across the screens of history
Discovered holy Buddha knelt in gentle prayer;
And marching on, Confucius the mighty one,
Compelling Eastern followers to contemplate.
So all-persuasive was their power, Edwin fell swayed,
And lingered long by these mystic tempting scenes
Of fixed serenity and idle certainty,
Contented there to dwell within those fragrant gardens.
Then Cheryl called, and broke the spell; rebuking him
With plucked notes from her old guitar. She strummed a
chord
Enticing harmony from simple stretched-gut strings
Lifting his reverie on humble music's wings.

The Spring Of Thought

VII

Cheryl held fixed the year, then spun location's dial
Transporting Edwin unto rapturous paradise:
The isle of Samos. Young and sweet with honeyed streams
Gushing cool and quiet past Queen Hera's temple;
Jealous wife of Zeus and Queen of Heaven, here honoured,
Till now returning honour through Pythagoras.
His boyhood heard the sea-strong rhythm's pounding
pulse;
While tuned lyre strings called softly to his ear,
And matched the plectrum nodes which Cheryl calmly
plucked:
Linked octaves, fifths or major thirds by length of string!
These pleasing harmonies and intervals of sound
Were held in perfect ratios– and by digits bound.

VIII

So small the step from music, to disgorge a law
And torch the cobwebbed timber of a secret realm;
For our earth might still encoat her sheen in beauty,
Or sprightly dance on insects' burnished wings; her tents
Could yet pour love and pride, emotion rage or joy
Into our hearts, or sink in deeps of mourning sorrow.
This movement of the strings graced movement in the
heavens–
Caught on crystal spheres to tinkle rhythmically.
The gods themselves came tumbling to this perfect wheel:
No fragment may escape when science wields his key;
Nor even may we hide in death's rough bloated grange–
Pythagoras taught, "All we know is number's range."

Girders in the Sand

IX

Embracing by eclectic power the hope of man,
Philosophy bade body, soul and mind unite;
Cosmology and medicine latched to counting frames
By fusing maths with music and that heavenly light,
Revealing sacred law in geometric form:
Religious pentagram and cabal rite conjoined
To natural number and the cosmic influence.
As triangle and squares could magic sides equate,
This axis-line of music bridged the far flung stars
Rekindling now in Titan's heirs that holy spark:
Ekstasis birthed through science in the conscious mind–
That music infinite, eternal, hence divine.

X

Through number's timeless dance the Brotherhood
achieved
Religious contemplation of the mysteries;
Attunement of the strings to intervals of scale
Brought spiritual release through cerebral delight.
Each fervent theorem conceived by mortal man
Marks his rebirth like some eternal deity.
Such science theories formed the wonders of the world,
Fresh-firing hope within the frame of all who seek
That greater, lasting world of deep, unending truth.
Geometry draws us away from worldly death:
Katharsis – purging of the soul, its pain removed;
Behold the 'ah' of art; the sigh of science loved.

XI

But from this Golden Height, which freed our globe to
slide
Among God's lamps with measured orbit, spin and weight,
Two men arose, who screwed it down again in clay:
The mystic, Plato, foe of natural science,
Thought: "All is shadow, without substance, grain or form.
Therefore, observing it by eye, no point is served,"
Condemning man to be shut up in caves again,
To watch but flickering shadows on the wall of life.
Next, Aristotle, arrogant observer, taught:
"Now all is known. Investigation can add naught
To what I have recorded. Change goes against God,
And hence is kept below heaven's luminary rod."

XII

Vainglorious, opinionated sorcerers!
Traducing Ptolemy to err by Plato's words:
"All motion must in perfect circles run," he said,
"To move at steady speed, their course lathe-turned in
Heaven."
While Aristotle took man from the farthest reach of God,
Constraining him within this inner sphere to die:
The Fall in permanence by devolution came,
With ultimate defeat below man's feet in Hell;
Above, 'The Prime Mover' lay locked beyond man's gaze.
With Christ, the breakdown was complete: the Dark Age
brought
Divorce of reason from belief, contempt for thought.

The Birth of the World

The days hung warm as summer spread
Her idle ways into the distant year.
A heavy green upon the boughs
Lulled swifts from tuneful readiness
Until a sudden eastern breath
Upon the wind chilled languishment
And forced them flee on fluted wings
To seasonal migration,
With final shrills to seek their way
Before the claw of winter's day.

Edwin too lingered from that year,
Wallowing in idleness,
Enjoying visits to the park
And teaching eager Mary-Anne
To wobble on her new-bought bike
Toward a road-edged freedom.
Of her mother, naught she asked
While Edwin kept the cuttings hid
Fearing truth might twist her mind
Or bruise her fragile love of him.

But Joy she knew of, and he spoke–
If pressed to– of that troubled day
He'd jilted cold tradition
Away– to rescue Mary-Anne!
Yet of perversity are made
The tumbling thoughts of childhood's hour,
Till she a rosy picture formed
Of myth and wild conjecture,
Idealised as missing mum:
That sensual, mythic woman lost
In lonely playgrounds of her mind.

The Spring Of Thought

Then Cheryl, arbiter of grief,
Suggested music as the sphere
To compass both her doleful gait
And his fresh need for learning.
And she too champed for music's lore:
In the wildness of her fingers,
In the tension of her being,
In the silence of her heart beat,
In the anguish of her longing,
Till grandparents moved to pity
Paid for tentative first lessons,
Giving her their old piano
With a shrug of unbelieving
At the power of her passion.

But, as swifts scent changing currents,
So he chilled through lack of income:
Fees for Cheryl's wise tuition
At the foothills of the giants.
And his parents stated that he
Should away, not fidget times fret;
Should concern himself with earning
Succour for the child's clothing,
Not to parrying her questions;
Should neglect that other region–
Where men search for hidden knowledge
Which may sleep beyond our waking
If infinity it yet spans,
Crossing thresholds of pure chaos,
Ending with destructive power
All the reasons we can offer
For a purpose to our living.

Wind howled, shouting round the roof beams;
Rain-lashed storms fought summer's end,

Girders in the Sand

Killing sleep with dreams excrescent,
Standing in a mortared city
Pruinate with desolation,
Portent of some greater loss:
Perhaps of youth, or innocence,
Or love given freely to a child,
Or madly claimed from woman's breast–
Lost for ever once its found.
Standing on this barren shoreline,
Where there'd been so great a loss,
Voices called from deep within him,
Echoing about the ruins,
Whispering between the pain,
"Think not of all that you have lost,
But of all you've yet to gain."
Then he turned once more to Cheryl,
To that temptress of the mind,
And resumed his daily studies
Of the earth from darkened skies.

Nothing seemed to men more rhythmic
Than the passing starry orbits
Turning on their wheels above them:
Clockwork spheres of driven crystal
Playing chords to who discern them.
Surely man must move beneath them
By their influence and guidance?
Edwin chose to match his learning
Of the passing starry motions
To a modern calculator,
So predicting man's blind passions
By the heaven's abject interest
On the sad affairs beneath them.
And he wrote a devious programme
On his new-loaned veraculem,

The Spring Of Thought

Taking dates and starry motions
To foretell the loves and interests
Of a clientele who flourished
From his prints of vague prediction.

Truly, he believed their power;
Who could gainsay what he thought?
Queues of people for the privilege
Of his fortunes sent their money,
And in this way did he prosper,
Tending Cheryl at her night class
To pursue the paths of heaven
Through a glassy compound eye.

The Wheel

Ptolemy (2nd Cent^y AD.)

O Ptolemy, astronomer maligned,
We know you for your wheels and perfect spheres;
Though with your star charts could Columbus find
A continent, yet through you grew our fears.

Your rigid, earth-locked system froze men's minds
With dread of change or stripping Christ's throne bare;
Your vision of perfected heaven blinds
Mankind, traducing truth – our rightful heir.

You culled the laws of physics from the sky,
Subjecting us to Inquisition's rod;
Your skilled designs hid all reality
While separating us from our true god.

      You strove so hard to save appearances,
      Yet left us naught, save incoherences.

          * * * * *

We share one common ancestry:
Till the final destiny,
  We but as children see.
From dread-filled night to sparkling day,
Life is motion in decay
  Through which we yearn to be.

The Timid Hero

Canon Copernicus (1473–1543)

Through hazy, damp grey vapours' swirling chill,
An omen crow descended silently
Then waited on a framing window stone,
Grey in grey mist about a weathered tower.
Hung far below, indifferent, unseen,
The citizens of Frouenberg awoke
To stretch and piss, to dress and take their bread
Or argue on a coin's toss their means,
Or toil about the business of the day;
Upon the tower none turned a caring eye.
None saw the crow cold-huddled, sentient there,
Nor spent one thought upon the man within–
A corpse still breathing, clammy cold he lay,
Awaiting death and full oblivion.

For two millennia, corpse-like as the priest,
Darkness of intellect had cloyed the air.
The light of reason, by gross umbra dulled,
Had atrophied through fear and bleak neglect,
Consigned so low, on heaven's Gold Chain acrouch.

His revered hero, Ptolemy, had claimed
That: "Physics of the skies is idle play,
For divine bodies different laws obey
And have no common links with earth's dull clay.
Astronomy is not reality."
Copernicus wished just to simplify
His hero's fixed, ungainly, rigid wheels
And spent his lifetime trying to reduce
Their number by a single cog or two
By taking out the motion of the sun

Girders in the Sand

About the earth. It wasn't fun,
For agonies of doubt assailed his mind
With fear of ridicule at what he'd done.
Medieval fetters pinioned spirit's verve
And strapped him, impotent to leave their bind.
By setting earth adrift, Copernicus
Became anarchic rebel to his God,
And bid to sit at Lucifer's right hand.
Decentralising man among the stars,
Donne's Little Mathematician trembled here:
For if a planet, planets too are worlds
And all elfin existence disappears.

Throughout the universe, from heaven to hell,
Democracy is cosmic in extent:
No absolute, no anchor up nor down,
No rigid cast– the Golden Chain was torn,
Anticipating revolution's fire
When all its tarnished links should be unborn.

Within his mind, the walled-in sanctuary
That framed medieval thought to finite ways
With limits set on knowledge, space and time,
Had cracked, revealing chasms through the rends
Insufferable in dark perplexity.
Infinity, with change eternal wrought,
Subquarried through the fabric of his world
More surely than would Luther's thunderous call.

For thirty lonely years he'd paused, unsure,
Afraid to print the contents of his mind
Until persuaded in his deathbed hour
To touch his manuscript, and sense its power.
To hope alone Copernicus now clung
With mantra chant of what had driven him:

The Timid Hero

"I kept the stars firm-fixed before my eyes
To rid posterity from ancient lies."

Inside the room, with new momentum gained,
The book fell from his hand till, tumbling slow,
It cracked the floor to stir the dusty silt
And startle up the waiting, glint-eyed crow.

Girders in the Sand

On the Death of his Father

Now summon up a scene of grim distress
      Where life is bleak and cold as driven rain.
      If you have wept and thought of the abyss
That brings extinction from unending pain
      Swept by a wind of ice, with aching limb,
      Head weak, enfeebled pulse and thrombosed vein,
Brow clammy sweat, eyes watering and dim,
      Then blend this livid scene onto your own.
      We walk toward the all-encircling rim
Whose cavern, death, looms like a monster grown
      Yet larger by absurd proximity
      To rob us of the treasures we have known.
To such a scene, with no proclivity,
      At three a.m. the telephone's loud toll
      Awoke Edwin in wild perplexity.
Unsure of husband's state, mum did cajole
      Her son to visit and lend youth's support,
      And thus he stepped into a night of coal
Where wind-tormented rain discomfort wrought,
      Cold coursing from his scalp with smarting lash
      To prise the eyes apart, then on it fought
In foamy rivulets before its dash
      About his neck and collar to his vest.
      Slow rolling thunder chased the lightning flash
As through drab streets he raced to childhood's nest
      And banged the door to face his mother's stare.
      Old Death stood waiting like an extra guest
Who knows his party piece with quiet flair,
      While others bustle ready for his show:
      A shadow making darkness blacker there;
A sudden shiver in the fire's glow.
      A retching cough demanded heed its sound:
      Expectorate, ancestral call, the foe

On The Death Of His Father

Of greater men, though stronger be not found
    Than Edwin's father, cursing slimy death
    As coward herald even while he drowned.
With hesitation worthy of Macbeth,
    His son crept trembling lead-foot up the stairs
    To find a wasted figure gasping breath,
While crawling dressing-gowned like one who dares
    Defy the world though all reason is done,
    Then falls, in noxious pools of vomitus.
Forth Edwin rushed, and scooped him like a son
    Into his arms; light as a babe he lay,
    Soft carried to his bed as he'd begun,
Their roles reversed like some transvestite play.
    Weak, slavering, unsure, eyes watering
    And crusted like a fly-blown weary dray,
Dad swore to keep the old fox loitering
    Until his bubbling breath turned words to blood.
    The fleecy pillow tempted smothering
To stem the hacking haem-flecked cough for good;
    He held it dagger high, till through the door
    His mother ran to break that frozen hood
Which masked his face, with frenzied agile claw.
    "What right have we to dictate death to those
    Who lie child-like in trust on our labour?
What unseen prejudice compels your blows?
    You extirpate your own fears, not his pain."
    Then Edwin fell as one whose sorrow grows
As they in battle who attend the slain;
    Guilt stricken, Edwin flannelled eyes and lips
    To catch his father's smile of firm disdain.
No simple man could breath through this eclipse,
    Though Edwin knew the sun behind its cloud
    Must glow as bright as ever without wisp,
And wondered if the mask was yet allowed
    To fall while thought searched heaven for a goal–

Girders in the Sand

But then the grizzled, craggy head snail bowed
As final life ebbed from its broken bowl,
     And all was still. The rictus expression
     Suggested swift release to stern parole
Rather than heaven's pleasant gestation.
     His woman sobbed, while Edwin bathed his face.
     The priest turned up with scant consternation,
Though sorry to be late, pronouncing grace
     Before the doctor came who named the death:
     "From pain, it was a merciful release;
His cancer grew to strangle every breath.
     Now he's at peace, and spared from further strife.
     Think not of tears, but the laughter he'd bequeath."
They moved downstairs, to celebrate his life
     With tea and cake, and talk of times now past,
     Till soon the carnival with jokes was rife,
With mother's picture albums flicking fast,
     Portraying history in black and white
     Until they went– then peace returned at last.
Through comatosing dreams of strange delight,
     Soft-billowing on forced, unbidden sleep,
     Old memories commanded that long night:
Of childhood days, and flippered-swimming deep
     Beneath a Cornish swell after a storm;
     Or carried shoulder high, too scared to weep,
Full snuggled in bronzed, brawny arms, blood-warm.
     Loud motorcycle rides to see a world
     Adventure-filled, with no push to conform,
And over all the scent of meadows swirled:
     Long walks on distant hills beside a stream
     To camp beneath the stars as bacon curled;
Songs out of tune, Al Jolson's jet sunbeam,
     And music-hall artistes long dead and gone,
     With half-remembered words, an aching dream,
But sung with gusto, tacking lyrics on.

On The Death Of His Father

The old pipe sucked through, packed with ash and tar,
And always, silly jokes for everyone:
Of cats with wooden legs who paced the bar
For beer, like beating Drake's old battle drum;
Or cannibals who called a taxi car
For meals on wheels, laced with a diesel rum.
He laughed and pranced through life as one with time;
He rarely drank, yet rarely sober seemed;
With button stakes, casino brag he'd mime,
And scoop the pot with chortled shouts, "My trick!"
The house was spotless, enemy to grime,
But curses reigned when paper would not stick,
Extruding slowly off the walls again.
That knee-wrenched dash to get the ball to kick;
A special treat, one night in London's rain,
Thick steaks, while best-suit smartly dressed.
Now stilled that voice, beyond reason's domain;
His family was his love, their lives his quest.
The hearse, ill-masked, in dying flowers hid,
Takes things unsaid and hopes unfilled to rest,
As earth slow rattles on the coffin lid.

21 May 1998

85

Orbital Duologue

Tycho de Brahe (1546–1601)
Johannes Kepler (1571–1630)

I

Through time our solemn song must gently turn
  The pages of the years to travel on;
Nigh sixty of them passed with scant concern
  For aught the timid Canon wrote upon;
His turgid book set no one's heart a-churn
  Until chance brought an annal baby, born
        In 1571, called Johanne Kepler,
        Upon the twenty-seventh of December.

II

In pretty Weil, in far-off Swabia
  (By stately Rhine and Forest Black it lies),
The child's mind flashed like cutting rapier.
  This herald nova, brillianting the skies,
None guessed as he pushed past the labia;
  There's no foretelling genius in a baby's cries.
        Wine-happy Weil would be forgotten now
        If that prem baby had not made his row.

Orbital Duologue

III

His father was an idle, drunken man
  Who took for bride the innkeeper's swart daughter,
A gruesome creature, quarrelsome of clan,
  Who used potents and herbs to try and flaunt her
Rites most magical, as only witches can–
  And to the witch's pyre it almost brought her.
      They tried to hang his father from a cart–
      Young Kepler had an inauspicious start.

IV

More miserable a childhood had no boy;
  A sickly child, with pasty face and mange,
Whose brutal father bullied him for joy;
  A swearing house, a smelling loathsome grange,
Complete antithesis to the Savoy,
  With aunts and uncles filled, all rather strange.
      At four, his wretched parents went to war;
      At nine to hard work bent, they were so poor.

V

Yet from this squalor, two small deeds recount
  The mother's love behind the evil tongue:
The earth sliced from the moon a fair amount,
  A comet with its tail wild-flaming, long
Across the sky, as nature's quoining fount.
  These things played in his mind as mother's song,
      As truth is claimed to be time's errant daughter,
      Or ducks are drawn to running, fish-stocked water.

Girders in the Sand

VI

Now some may question why a titchy child
  Should skyward find release for fevered brain;
Eclipses of the moon are somewhat mild,
  While comets come and go without restrain.
Perhaps they checked a childhood life rent wild
  Like an umbrella checks cold drizzly rain;
      Or isles in flooding fields give sanctuary,
      Or Yanks seek solace from their attorney.

VII

Of he whose path would orbit Kepler's rock,
  A silver spoon adorned his mouth, and more.
Named Tycho Brahe, from noble Danish stock,
  His father governed close to Elsinor;
Yet he, too, faced a childhood psychic shock
  When kidnapped by his uncle for a score.
      This admiral had no children of his own,
      So took his brother's child as ready grown.

VIII

This uncle foster-father turned to weeds
  As many sailors do, through too much water.
Returning from a battle 'gainst the Swedes,
  The king's horse thought there'd been too little slaughter
So tried to add the king's death to his deeds
  By sliding on a bridge's icy mortar.
      The king fell headlong in the stream below;
      The admiral leapt to save him from the flow.

Orbital Duologue

IX

Alas, he saved his king, but lost his life
  From chills encountered in that frosty moat.
It took three days of fierce, remorseless strife
  Before he slipped away his earthly coat.
Young Tycho ended up with just the wife,
  Who cared not on this cuckoo child to dote.
      She packed him off to university,
        With hopes he might a noble statesman be.

X

A rival noble Danish youth had claimed
  That maths could be advanced by brute contest.
Thus came the spat for which he's over famed–
  A duel to ascertain which answered best.
They fought for knowledge, and Tycho was maimed,
  With nose sliced off, to show his brain was blessed.
      For truth, like honour, beauty, wealth and right
        Falls victim when the only judge is might.

XI

To make amends for his lost gallant conk,
  He made a monolith of beaten gold;
A cubist nose, with loud metallic honk,
  Which ageless shone, while he grew old and bald.
Forever polished, yet forever cold,
  One cough would scythe all, like a raiding stonk;
      His nose became his constant inspiration,
        Anointed daily with an embrocation.

Girders in the Sand

XII

Why should a dilettante Danish fop
  From wealth and leisure seek exactitude?
The ticking clocks of gold in heaven's backdrop
  Pushed him to spurn a life of rectitude.
As Greek-predicted star charts were a flop,
  He vowed to bring some Danish certitude;
      He made a quadrant built of brass and oak–
      A thirty-six foot monster to his yoke.

XIII

He fathered modern scientific way
  By measuring to fractions of a minute.
Till Tycho, Aristotle's rule held sway:
  "The laws of heaven lie beyond our limit;
One measure will unchanging stars display;
  Three points a circle's circumference delimit."
      Precision for precision's sake became
      His sole religion, and deserved fame.

XIV

Three times in Tycho's life the heavens spoke:
  Once, when the sun was hid, his heart had leapt;
Again, when planets in conjunction broke
  The acquiescing silence that had morphic crept
Into men's minds a thousand years, and woke
  Him to the errors that these savants kept;
      Third, a supernova glowed where none had been;
      Not since Hipparchus had new stars been seen.

Orbital Duologue

XV

Young Tycho fixed its bearing to the inch;
  He proved it did not move by one hair's breadth,
Which put God's institutions in a pinch
  From fear it signalled rigid church's death,
For new stars make old theologians flinch
  And several had to draw in deeper breath:
          "Immutable, the cloth of heaven should be—
          Change breaks perfection, and eternity."

XVI

A supernova is a marvellous sight—
  The brightest death throes in the universe,
Which spawns new forms of matter to ignite
  Young stars, and planets' people who converse
Of dire omens. Their prodigy delight
  As seeds whom parents celebrate in verse,
          Though none of this could Tycho then surmise;
          His main delight was watching changing skies.

XVII

On hearing of young Tycho's reputation,
  King Frederick, who'd recovered from his plunge,
Sent messengers to ride across the nation
  With offers of a huge estate to sponge
For income through the power of degradation
  (Perhaps he wished the admiral to expunge).
          Bold Tycho built upon the isle Hveen
          The largest astro-tower the world had seen.

XVIII

So Tycho came, with fulsome retinue
  Of servant girls to fill each bath and whim,
A jester-dwarf to play the Fool when blue,
  Dumb sycophants, fat cooks, three carvers trim,
A train of tailors bearing cloth to view;
  All idled time, like ladies at a gym.
            His tame elk drank the beer and fell down stairs,
            To end up as a mention in his prayers.

XIX

Though gazing then was without telescope
  (That gift had Galileo yet to know),
For twenty years he laboured, full of hope,
  A mistress and his children down below,
And fine appearances above to cope
  With aristocracy's vain fur and flow.
            A thousand stars touched by his astrolabe
            Were etched in steel upon a giant globe.

XX

His personal life was lived as feudal lord.
  Such grand hauteur bred insolent disdain
Which festered through his subjects as discord;
  He'd shackle helpless families to a chain,
For flouting trivial laws or tax ignored–
  Then lock them in his dungeon for their pain,
            Till forced to distant exile by his Prince;
            Cruel arrogance makes moderate despots wince.

Orbital Duologue

XXI

For Kepler, geometry was God himself,
  Inherent in the world when time began.
Astronomers, who ladle heaven's wealth,
  Interpret nature's laws like priests to man,
While horoscopes on Reason rule by stealth,
  Directing our affairs with sweet élan.
          But priests, who read this book of Nature's Laws,
          Ought have the right to answers for each clause.

XXII

His friends selected carelessly a wife–
  A stupid, sulking, ailing Xanthippe,
Twice widowed daughter of a miller's life
  Who nagged her husband's work with asses' bray.
Her dowry brought more enmity and strife
  Into this lowly teacher's joyless day.
          Instead of friends' advice to tie the rope,
          Young Kepler should have used his horoscope.

XXIII

From pulpits, warring clerics screamed blue oaths
  Like fishwives, or his vile parents before.
He would not doff the Lutheran faith he chose,
  Though fined for walking through a churchyard door
Bearing his daughter to her grave's repose;
  The Catholic duke was narrow on that score.
          Kepler kept Luther's vows, through beadledom:
          "Keep faith, and shun hypocrisy's soft drum."

Girders in the Sand

XXIV

Yet through these timeless, splenic, holy wars
  Where priests donned righteous garb to vent their cant,
Young Kepler held that geometric laws
  Reflected God in worlds more permanent,
Existing before man, and at death's pause;
  To crack them would be truly excellent.
        Five perfect solids, regular in shape,
        In orbit locked five planets from escape.

XXV

Alas, his orbits had an ugly look;
  Fresh data were required to ease their strain,
And none could better those that Tycho took,
  So Kepler vowed to plunder his great brain.
Gruff Tycho, much impressed by Kepler's book,
  Now asked the tyro to attend his train.
        So when, at last, Kepler was forced to flee,
        He rode to Tycho's court with open glee.

XXVI

To orbit like a comet, Kepler came,
  First cautiously as often moves the poor,
Adducted by the power of might and name,
  Held captive by the treasure through that door;
Pulled as by gravity to Tycho's fame,
  He vowed to wrest Mars' orbit from his maw.
        So each with each outvied to cut the knot
        Which hid the curves on which the planets trot.

Orbital Duologue

XXVII

And then, oh woe! embarrassing to tell,
  While feasting with nobles of high office,
And Jepp the sultry Fool played one last knell,
  Old Tycho drank too much and could not piss
So took to bed with belly like a bell.
  For days he dangled over the abyss
        And begged his life might not have seemed in vain;
        So Kepler stole his notes to ease his pain.

XXVIII

He struggled for eight years with stubborn facts
  Through countless sheets of complex algebra
By troving Tycho's golden data racks,
  Computing perfect circles round our star.
"Who would have thought it possible," he cried,
  "That this hypothesis, though on a par
        With observed oppositions Tycho found
        Is nevertheless false. The shape's not round!"

XXIX

Through eight years work, the ruthless facts remained
  To taunt him with eight minutes tiny arc.
A lesser hero might such facts disdain–
  Such lesser heroes love life in the dark.
But Kepler would not Tycho's wealth profane
  So struggled till one shape at last stood stark.
        One curve keeps Kepler's repute from eclipse:
        "It's not a circle– this thing's an ellipse!"

Girders in the Sand

XXX

But publishing, as many authors know,
  Is oft beset with problems on the way.
The heirs of Tycho now became the foe
  With eyes for gold, but set in minds of clay.
While tussling over who should run the show
  They locked the instruments and notes away.
        The instruments decayed to worthless scrap;
        These little problems can delay a chap.

XXXI

Theology needs strong Authority
  Whose weight will light the faith lent by God's word;
But noble logic rules philosophy,
  And Reason is the voice which should be heard.
Though saints may suffer much atrocity,
  Their rule on planets' movements seems absurd.
        The Holy Office stated: "Earth is fixed;"
        But Kepler prayed: "Let Law with Truth be mixed."

XXXII

Capricious fate, meanwhile, sent many slings
  To frustrate Kepler's struggle for the stars.
His mother tried to fly on witch's wings
  Till held for trial, constrained by man's cruel bars
And threatened with the stake. Such trying things
  Disturb attempts to find orbits for Mars.
        When geometric models must be made,
        Despair and darkness lend an urgent blade.

Orbital Duologue

XXXIII

Now plagues and bitter war made Kepler weep;
  Prague lay at siege, his wife and child atomb.
His house, built on the outer city sweep,
  Was filled with soldiers ramming flame and fume
And boom of cannon, breaking work and sleep,
  As others stole lead from his printer's room.
          Rebelling peasants tried the town to raze,
          And learned books burn with a heady blaze,

XXXIV

While Kepler, without irony or mock,
  The *Harmony of the World* wrote for delight,
Whose granite base formed Newton's solid rock.
  Through anguished grit the last law came to light:
Once more he had to flee, or face the block,
  And wandered like the Jew from night to night.
          With modest understatement for these frays,
          He said, "some incidents had caused delays."

XXXV

All thoughts of perfect circles were now axed,
  Liberating thought for our rebirth;
The sun itself was displaced to the backs,
  A focus, not the centre, of our girth.
And he, who touched the planets in their tracks,
  Set down his anchor in the quiet earth.
          Yet even death turned Kepler's restless lathe;
          The War of Thirty Years dispersed his grave.

Girders in the Sand

The Dream of Vetulus

Galileo Galilei (1564–1642)

"…. Who seeks
To lessen Thee, against his purpose serves
To manifest the more thy might; his evil
Thou usest, and from thence creat'st more good."
John Milton, *Paradise Lost*, Book VII.

Here I lie, a blind man in an arid time,
Melded to this world by one unyielding past,
remembering.

What fruit bears triumph now to moist these corded lips;
What 'scope brings power of vision to these rheumy orbs?
My God, who gave me peerance power, has scorched my eyes;
My church, for all eternity, has fed disharmony.
And I, once damned by God, now damned by man,
Lie frozen in a dusty land.

Saint Lucy, throw your pennate beams
For pity through this soul-encloying dark;
Here I see no future passage through unforgiving time
Nor present ease to torment; only bitter past
Which stops my eyes with ceaseless tears.
What joy is knowledge caged or thought confined?
Verbigeration drives these questions round
Through endless circles to involve us all;
And always haunting, haunting, Bruno's end,
Their own whipped cur who dared aver
That Heaven's extent should match our God.

The Dream Of Vetulus

And in old age I dream of youth
And smell stale dust within the school
Where I was set to be a priest,
Save for my father's will.
I hear once more songs that he played,
Strident in their novel sound,
Rebellious to ancient form.

To plague humanity with irksome truth,
To set us all adrift about a poxy sun
By plucking from the hearth of God this little earth
Must shake the bravest heart's imaginings.
To pull rebellious music from the moon,
To widen in a moment mankind's gaze
Beyond fixed spheres; to plumb the cloistered depths
Of infinite black emptiness, whose rays,
Enfeebled by such passages, became
First visible to man, was glorious.

In the yard the papal spies pace back and fro,
Blocking contact with my friends,
And ointment for my eyes.
Here, even pigeons have a peck that scars
And I, who once debated Dante's Hell,
Know its wide circles and the Sixth Terrain too well.

In that dread chamber with unspoken Holy threat,
I smelt the acrid fumes seep through my rebel sweat.
If, disobedient to His strong will, I railed,
To that great depth, whose penalty is hope curtailed,
I must descend. By torn pathways steep and fickle,
Through the choking smoke which smothers that foul circle,
I see the burning tombs which no man's tears can quell.
Untenanted, one tomb ablaze in deepest hell
Is gaping to receive one condemned member more:

Girders in the Sand

This excommunicant and heretic at law.
And thus the sickly hue of rampant cowardice
Clay-paints my trembling lips above that great abyss.

One supreme man has now transfixed the earth,
Unturning, rigid in his cramped cosmos:
Roberto Bellarmine. That small saint
Who scrubbed the scullery of his bleak cell
And lived the poverty that others vow,
For whom, compared to God and His bright eye,
The glory of the heavens were not great;
Who shook their very beauty with contempt,
At death was mobbed by crowds who relics craved;
While I die here, back-broken and alone.
That finest flower of learning in our church
Fought science as he fought the Protestants:
With zealous faith and fixed, unbending will;
But by insisting that to say "It moves"
Is heresy, prohibited and damned,
What swamps he breeds for all in Holy Church,
If braver men shall ever prove its truth.

That passionate defender of the faith
Unfazed by doubt, for whom perversity
Held dread more dire than fearful plagues could sow,
Confronted and confounded my attempts
To show that Holy Scripture does not err.
Yet Nature too cannot transgress her Law,
Nor cares one whit for understanding times.
The Bible has no word on planets' ways,
And leaves their orbits to the mind of men.
To use base scripture to interpret facts
Which might, with time, conclude another way,
Debases dignity and hidden faith.
To take as literal that lofty text

The Dream Of Vetulus

Has censored science and our mutual sense.

Emprisoned in this desiccated cell,
Each wince affirming threatened rack or screw,
I wait for news to percolate these walls
Ashake with terror least they come anew.
Uncompromising terror from lost hope
Pervades the rigid realms of ritual man;
Yet Faith with Science, once entwined again,
Will break the Inquisition's most unholy plan.

Young Milton called, whose sober words
Admixed contempt with pity for my state,
Before returning to some civil strife.
He writes and travels widely as he picks
And talks of freedom in that English realm
To scrawl or discourse to his mind's dictate;
Our choking flattery and fustian
May serve to fire his rebel pen to march.
I hear his voice is if he's in my brain:
Though free, yet full of fury 'gainst his king.
Some spark, perhaps, he'll take to kindle there:
From imminent death, some freer, brighter blaze.
But with my death dies Italy's last hope;
Her voice to slighter subjects must now turn
And silence will reign here on matters deep.

Girders in the Sand

I, knowing knowledge grows with spreading time,
Who added to that store of splendid lore
New moons, and craters none had seen before,
With certain knowledge know I will exchange
My present prison for that narrow one
Which long endures, and which awaits us all.

To pen me down by these garlanded gates,
Authority, in crabby purple dress,
Has wielded its might to wild effect.
Slow smouldering, 'neath gross iniquity,
Hard-yoked to that censorious edict,
In pity bound to full obedience,
I wait my end.

And yet– authority cohesion brings
To lives fragmented by such diverse streaks,
And pulls intemperate thought to conjoined whole.
What wars, invasions, pestilence and disarray
Befall us once authority is flouted
And right of Law suspended by base rule,
As Rome once saw, and England sees again.
Outside obedience struts anarchy,
Dictatorship and desolation's door.
Once cut from Mother Church, what chaos looms,
With fragmentation wild in disarray,
A myriad of Protestant profusion,
Foreboding bloodshed in the tussled earth.
Though undiscovered, Nature's Law and plan
Controls us all; no less must civil law
Dictate our acts, while sweet obedience
Conforms our once beleaguered souls to God.

The Dream Of Vetulus

None born in civil fields is wholly free,
Unless head of some barren anarchy;
All bow to some Law, subject to some king,
Controlled by others, and by force unknown.
Obedience alone lets freedom grow,
And following authority, our lives
May stroll in verdured lanes with quiet peace,
Untroubled by fresh thought or gloomy doubt.

And yet– authority itself can err:
Authority, from Aristotle's pen,
Has bound our universe with petty walls;
Authority, from wrongful ruler's sword,
Will rip as gentle breast as ever breathed;
Authority set Christ upon the cross
And ordered simple nails to weapons yield;
Injustice was defied by Dante's hand,
Till– banished by authority– he died.
And every step of learning must defy
The fundamental truths that went before.

And therein lies the pain of paradox–
For as a child I burst my bonds to stretch
Beyond the confines of my father's house
And leave my mother's warmth and tenderness;
Now I contain the essence of revolt
To leave the strictures of a rigid past
And break for regions new and insecure.
How weak must be this dressed authority,
Which fears the pen may strip it of its garb;
Exposure holds no fear for certainty;
Tradition's robes may mask doubts plenary.

Now so near death, I see their fear;
Yet my fear lies not in idle death, but hell:

Girders in the Sand

To be cut off from God, abhorred, outcast,
Anathema to Holy Mother Church,
Has more of dread than truth suspended.
This bleak dulosis reeks of rotten choice:
To scorch in briefest agony
And face God's slow damnation,
Or change eternal for this earthly hell?
Under what stratagems do I so bake?
Science is not faith, to stand or fall on martyrs' backs;
Against such accusations I must stand alone.

Alone– and ever silent to their sneers;
The sarcasms and insults that they hurl
I swallow with no chance of slaked assault.
I might hope for a pardon if I'd erred;
Because I have committed no offence,
To free me broadcasts their more deadly guilt.
Alone– and yet perpetually called
By my beloved daughter's anguished plea,
That gentle nun, beyond the solemn grave
Yet calling still, with muffled prayer for me.
She wrote of simple things in Arcetri;
Of selling lemons for a holy mass,
Recited in her convent for my soul.
I took bouquets across the Tuscan hills
To bring a bloom of sun to her drab cell.

Conflict, deep love and longing made her ill;
Reciting Penitential Psalms each week,
And full of hope, with laughter in her eyes,
She even took my penance on herself,
Until she died within her cloister walls,
That winter when the roses bloomed in snow.
Now, frost in summer chills each fragrant bloom
As canker, curl, and rot their scent consume.

The Dream Of Vetulus

Beneath a coat in summer heat I lie,
Too weak to shiver, yet too strong to die.
I feel my God lives closely by your hand
And wonder if the world will understand.

Girders in the Sand

The Temple of King Solomon

Isaac Newton (1642–1725)

Gaunt, alone, near nothing, stands
Woolsthrope Manor where was born,
after his father died,
  A solitary boy, selfishly abandoned
By remarriage of his mother.
He fought within himself
To master learning,
To struggle as a servant in the college halls,
To battle with intolerant religion,
Circumstance of regal rule,
Contemporaneous adversaries,
And bewildering, disjointed Nature's law.
Alone, for ever alone, he lived and worked and died;
But to his mind, populous more than any foggy fenland town,
From biblical antiquity stirred rousing savants
To hoop his hidden scaffold-building alchemy.

The temple of King Solomon,
Built to a holy plan, on blood-stained ground
Already sacred to these warring tribes
Before records began,
Gave plans both pivotal and unctuous.

There, at the heart of its most secret chamber,
Glowed a flame eternal,
Central to the mystic host, fed for sacrifice,
A faith-proclaiming symbol of their everlasting, unseen god,
God both of birth and battle,
Of salvation, hope and death,
Of wealth given, and sacrifice taken and expected.

The Temple of King Solomon

Next, cradled round, the stone-cold chamber
Of fawning priests and acolytes
Circumferencing the sanctum,
Restrained by awe, yet central drawn to this one sacred flame.
Peripheral to all, to chambers, courts and wall,
The common man, distant
Yet eternal,
An unchanging constancy, buttressed by the brief span
Of each quiescing life.

Thus he dissipates his hours until, upon the dying day,
He sits sequestered in a darkened room
Refining Ezekiel's vision of the long-dead prophet,
Solomon– in Newton's eyes the wisest of the wise–
Perfecting sketches of a temple built
Three thousand years before.
Each word and line vivid as a cut in stone,
Bright as blazing light flashed through a window slat,
Imaged firm within his head where here the prophet lives.
Each stone, real and granite cold,
Traced with mental fingers through the mason's cracks,
Cut crystal sharp and hard.

And from this studied alchemy grows out
A stronger vision to supplant the ancient paradigm:
Of fiery sun's eternal flame, and planets held
In courtly dance around a hallowed central fire,
Drawn ever in, as apples are earth-drawn,
Yet constantly flung out through space
By their innate momentum.

Two thoughts threading through the life of man,
Two diverse homilies in one eternal plan:
Motion in the heavens, described by Kepler's law,
And motion here on earth, which Galileo saw,

Girders in the Sand

Each one held in lone community,
Now merge in Newton to a marvellous unity.
He saw repeated order in the galaxies and sun;
The movement of a distant star within a marble's run.

In Kensington, at Mary Abbot's church,
Where once he worshipped when success had come,
How apt the homily in stained glass held,
Plucked from the Book of Kings as epitaph.
For "Let the shadow return backwards" says
More of alchemy than rational science;
And bridging worlds irrational and wild
With order tamed and factually displayed
Shall stand as epitaph, this King of science crowned,
Who dared to dream – and dreaming, dared to sing.

On Learning of Einstein

Albert Einstein (1879–1955)

If Manitou the Mighty once moved his braves to war;
If thrice the scared groves have held a baton for our score;
If power of song can grip you upon its timeless wing
To sense a moment of delight as more than just you sing;
If any age has pulled you to thoughts you do not own
To know alone we do not live, but always share the throne
Of heaven with battalions who once did march before,
And retrospective others who will follow through your door;
If flesh observed while living conceals the moulding bone,
Or love can push you past the gate of logic to its own,
You may have felt a tremor, worlds moving out of sight,
Of shadows playing far beyond the rim of silent night;
This is the cry of freedom, this is the end to pain,
This anodyne anointing balm which gives eternal reign
To circumstance and jesting on which the rest hold play,
To what moves oft beyond the mind, yet holds us in its sway.

How shall I dare express it? Ideas that fly as birds
When given algebraic wing, plummet to earth as words.
Eternal notes in symbols require an elegy
That I, with simple pen, lack rhyme or rhythm to set free;
This huge, heroic figure, whose world seems far apart,
Could conquer Himalayan peaks yet keep a modest heart.

Some fields of his the world knows: of relativity,
And that bizarre equivalence twixt mass and energy.
Can light eject electrons? He first described the way,
For which effect the Nobel prize came under his wan sway.
Yet quantum physics fooled him; that magic isle so small,
Wherein the coins of Nature's bank finance the atom's stall.

Girders in the Sand

For Heisenberg, Schrödinger and Bohr chance added spice,
To which he famously remarked, "My God does not play
dice."
Now Einstein took a wrong path, and all his final years
Were spent at futile error's door– neglected by his peers–
For in the realm of man's thought, effect and cause both sing,
But deep within the atom's core blind chance alone is king.

Fantastic is the music that struggles 'gainst the past,
Complete in form, invariable, eternally set fast;
Just so each wave of knowledge, with its rewarding praise
Averring awe in Nature's Law, continues to amaze.
Yet all this hard-won knowledge yields not the final look
But words– whose sounds delight us all, while we ignore the
book.

In Music's Power

Beyond The Mind

The fruits of life are rich, yet all decay
To shadows which confound the richest hall;
And morrow circles round the brightest day—
That nameless sorrow which surrounds us all.

Though some may doubt the ceaseless march of time
And hold that books are nothing more than ink,
With art and science, or the poet's rhyme,
But reflex gestures in time's tiny blink,

If there be more than rotting flesh to death,
If music's power can soar on timeless helm,
If ever spirit stirred with softest breath
To hint of hidden point or purple realm,

Two gifts shall keep us from the world apart:
The prize of intellect; a hopeful heart.

* * * * *

What if the way be long and steep,
Or the river flows too deep?
  Shall we be overwhelmed?
From speculation of our start,
Contemplate this final part—
  Then reach the higher ground.

Girders in the Sand

In Music's Power

I

At last, that season cycles round again
Which tempts the young to bike beyond their doors
With hopes that scattered clouds don't portend rain,
While parents pack their picnics for sand floors.
Entrepreneurs, meanwhile, dust well-known scores
And hire parks, marquees and trinket stalls,
Preferring lakes and boats with lighted oars,
Then book an orchestra's alfresco calls,
Performing for their throng, away from concert halls.

II

Now gather clans for kinship, feast and fray,
With wicker chairs, wide baskets filled with food,
Lead glass asparkle in the fading day,
And simple candle lamps to set the mood
Beneath broad tents to shade the wealthy brood–
Ample to house a horse and stately knight.
About the beer tents, poorer mortals queued
For crisps and flagons worthy of their plight;
These thronging groups of colour form a pretty sight.

In Music's Power

III

Brass, strings, and wind assembled on the stage
In curving ranks of sombre evening gowns;
An orchestra built up from youth's fresh age,
And limited to girls from local towns,
Who rose to greet their leader, then sat down–
Until their conductor appeared behind–
A feminist, ferocious and renowned,
Whom critics have too frequently maligned,
While being to her genius somehow deaf and blind.

IV

Applause now rippled round the gathered crowd,
Who stayed from nibbling to observe her mien;
A woman whose close-cropped red hair endowed
Her high-boned face with russet sheen;
A band of pearls embraced her brow's demean,
Matching those set about her narrow throat.
She poised, arching her brows above the scene
Of merrymakers, then appeared to float
Her arm in liquid air– which splashed to her first note.

V

Her theme was England, played in dream and song–
Elgar's *Chanson de Nuit*, Holst's *Planet Suite*,
Then Tippett's startling cascades, tumbling long,
Surprising as a waterfall's glist sheet
Wild splashed in azure lake from rocky leet.
The Few from Walton's score she drew more stark:
A Spitfire overhead circled its beat–
Drawn in a wartime searchlight's blazing arc–
Then rolled and looped in cartwheels high above the park.

Girders in the Sand

VI

With closing summer's day, a chill breeze blew
To blush the cheek during *Jerusalem*,
Performed by one who wore red, white and blue,
Full power-voiced – a real soprano gem.
The conductor she'd known since common stem
At school, continuing good bosom friends
Through music school, which laid the road for them.
And music, too, blooms best from common trends,
While future buds appear from what the present lends.

VII

To the right side, upon the stage, sat low,
With long, black dress and shoulder-tressing hair,
Caressing as a lover her cello,
Her eyes half closed, as though not wholly there,
Yet breathing rhythm like some noble air
That gave her being life more meaningful,
A young girl stroked her bow with skilful flair.
She played her forte with a thunder-full
Effect – her passion for the piece was wonderful.

VIII

It ended with a firework flare above
To celebrate through gaudy burst's bellow,
Which hit the night peace like a boxer's glove–
While Joy encased with care her fine cello.
Across the park, lit in the dark, sat low,
A child was staring fixedly at her–
Then seemed to tug the sleeve of some odd fellow
Who turned and glared, which set her mind astir,
And set her heart apounding with an iron burr.

In Music's Power

IX

Joy turned to leave discretely from the stage
And stepped out from the platform's rear-most door,
But in her haste she managed to misgauge
Its height, and sprawled, entangled, on the grassy floor.
Her cello slid aside, her shin was grazed and sore
With mud and dirt where nylons once had been;
Her hair knotty as any complex law;
One shoe was shied and nowhere to be seen,
When from the darkness called the girl: "You need a clean!"

X

With battered apprehension, Joy stared up
To see against the flames the young girl's face.
She skitted like a frisky new-born pup,
Then rushed to help Joy up with firm embrace,
Before retrieving, first, the cello case
Handled with care, then next the grass-stained shoe.
Joy settled on the step to thread its lace,
While dancing round with glee the young girl flew
And said, "I would have looked for ever, just for you."

XI

Behind the shadowed tent, Edwin had slunk,
Embarrassed least by Joy he was reviled.
But Joy from gentle mannered cups had drunk,
And standing said, "So you must be Jane's child."
The girl picked up the cello unbeguiled,
"Oh no," she cried, "I'm yours– you're my step-mum."
Snatching the case, her breathing now grown wild,
Joy ran from answering, her thoughts were dumb,
While down her cheeks the tears of bitterness had come.

Girders in the Sand

XII

She turned, her face a ghostly, firework green
Which flickered as her turmoil pulsed with hate.
Her loathing for this man had grown more keen
As each crabbed anniversary's marked slate
Had mocking come and left her single state.
Him seeing now, she wanted to fling mud,
But screamed her anger– pent within for eight
Long years of silent tears and burning blood–
Now burst in wounding, savage words its damned-up flood.

XIII

Her passion spent, her tongue composed and still,
She walked eye-bright, head high, away– then turned
With bare contempt for what reply he'd trill,
But in her heart her anger still fierce burned.
Ignoring Mary-Anne, whose love she'd spurned
And who now blanched at the riposte she'd heard–
(Who for a missing mother's love had yearned)
Joy strode the night without a further word;
Her genial nature had by now grown somewhat blurred.

XIV

Her rooms were dark when she returned, alone–
Dark as her anger, black as bitter mood–
From knowing Edwin, eight sad years had flown.
She played some Bach for solace, and to brood;
In sensual notes drawn deep, from heaven hewed,
Her restless mind with solemn visions filled,
Which calmed her pulse and gave her fortitude:
On distant moors a brook snaked, heather-hilled,
Soft plashing boulders– where a circling hawk had killed!

In Music's Power

XV

Then faster beat the frenzied, pulsing strings;
Her hand pulled sharply to imagined blow
With quavers soaring as the hawk's stiff wings
To plunge with swift descent on death below.
Her mind returned to time– long aches ago–
When music lit her life and led her dance
Adroitly with a ballet-gliding bow.
Pursuing early talent was luck's chance;
But love had died– a victim preyed on by romance.

XVI

Then Bridget entered, ruddy cheeked and cross–
With wheezy breathing like a village pump,
Her pungent mood a cleansing burning joss.
Her eyes aglaze, her figure slightly plump,
She threw her violin down in a hump.
"You forgot to bring me home," at last she gasped,
Which brought Joy to the moment with a bump.
"I need a drink!" said she, telling what elapsed.
"But that girl's at the gate," said Bridget, as Joy collapsed.

XVII

But even as she fell, the door bell chimed.
Joy lay– a trembling aspen to so slight a breeze,
While Bridget fumed and thought it all ill-timed.
Joy clawed for air, half choking half a wheeze,
And weakly stretched for Bridget's sleeve to seize.
She cried with passion, "No! Don't let her in!"
Hysteria like this can never please,
But to her whim she went, despite the din,
Though such a state precipitates a head-long spin.

Girders in the Sand

XVIII

Returning, Bridget simply said, "She's gone."
Becalmed by this, Joy poured the second drink
As Bridget sat beside and gave her tongue,
Berating Joy who should enact, not sink
Her duty to divorce this male-made stink.
"You've never squared to what was done," she said,
"You've turned to pent-up pain a Nelson's wink.
From your tight mouth, we'd think you'd never wed;
You have to live before you're named among the dead."

XIX

Joy bit her lip and gulped from inner pain,
But Bridget would not silenced be by rage,
Relating how, when truth becomes a stain,
Exposure is the bleach that will assuage.
"Your love and life must grow on music's page;
This crook-backed state has held you back from fame–
Your destiny's to walk a solo stage.
From thoughts about that man, ditch every claim;
Now let the cello's calling be your only aim."

XX

"You have a greater gift, in flare and style,
Than anything my violin can weave.
Your playing has the power to beguile;
This gig tonight is all I will achieve.
For years, yourself you've failed to believe;
Now grow anew, it's time to purge the past.
You have more passion than man can conceive–
Except with muddied pity its bound fast.
Tomorrow night, that fouled-up anchor you will cast."

XXI

Next day, Joy looked a pitiable sight:
Hair wild, eyes glazed, teeth coated like old cheese;
Her head the empty bottle from the previous night.
Bridget pumped aspirin to annul the lees
And opened windows for a cleansing breeze.
Joy shuddered slightly, for her leg had flopped
As myriad ants crawled up, her skin to seize.
She sat at table with her head hand-propped,
And thought, "This self-destructive flensing must be stopped."

XXII

"I've told the girl to come back here today;
She needs to see you to address the past,
And you must face your fire, not run away,
Before this conflagration turns to blast.
Now here she comes, you stay– don't look aghast–
While I arrange some tea and clear the room."
So Mary-Anne came in, her eye downcast,
But willing still some contact to resume,
Though knowing now Joy's love she never could assume.

XXIII

Ignoring Joy, the young girl hid unease
Within the niche where a piano stood.
Her fingers kissed so softly on the keys,
Though moving stiffer than a Grade Five should;
Her passion for the piece moved through the wood
Till, like a miracle of falling rain
Down-pouring on a desert sand for good,
A cello air took up the sweet refrain:
A slow duet of peace and promise born through pain.

Girders in the Sand

XXIV

The music's swell and fall brought tides of balm
To which, in rapturous floods, Joy's bow did bend;
Cascades of triplets presaged endless calm
Full flowing, though the child petered an end.
Stopped notes in wave on wave can apprehend
A moment and a mood in time to pause,
As wild melodic limestone blocks append
A gritty structure to their barren moors;
Then, in the final silence, came a child's applause.

XXV

Joy smiled – and in that moment, time sloughed off
Depression's weight and ageing bitterness
As though the devil'd ridden her enough;
And with that smile of welcome openness,
The child ran to her side with sweet caress
And wrapped her longing arms about Joy's neck.
Her touch was like a massage, easing stress,
Which time had long laid heavy on her deck,
Until it streamed away at this girl's cooling beck.

XXVI

Within that moment cracked the mental bind,
And Joy rushed to embrace the simple child.
As summer's warmth displaces winter's grind,
Soft words slipped through where once the tongue ran
wild;
Sweet praise for days which once had been reviled.
Too soon the moment ceased: the cello stilled,
Whose sintered notes held Mary-Anne beguiled,
Old images flashed back– a mother killed–
Till love destroyed the lathe on which their hate was milled.

In Music's Power

XXVII

Gloved power subsists in music to disarm—
Yet shifts in tempo move us to attack.
Once soft-bowed strings exude celestial balm,
From hell what subtle songs may bring us back?
A woven cloth of fugal gold by Bach,
Before whose rhythm rampant hate demurred;
Such harmony strikes light from awesome black
By touching depths no conscious mind has heard—
Its power pulsates beyond the reach of any word.

XXVIII

So rage gave way to pleasure, work, and pain,
As Joy rebuilt her musical career.
Long practice lead to prizes once again,
For Bridget laid a course for her to steer—
A steady road to which she could adhere.
Though Mary-Anne called regularly now,
From Edwin conversation had to veer;
But snippets filtered through: enough to plough,
By thought of him, to puzzled furrows her young brow.

XXIX

The simple shopkeeper she'd known had gone:
A man phlegmatic, humble, yet bemused,
Had devastated all he'd gazed upon.
All knowledge gained has left successors bruised,
Though advocates for change have long enthused
The virtue in each modern thought or thrill.
But science left Joy ever more confused;
Music alone contains the power to still
This life's cacophony, when Stentor blows too shrill.

Girders in the Sand

XXX

Perhaps through passion, yet perhaps through pain,
About this time Joy "saw the light of God"
And sensed a new life enter her own brain,
As Bridget's constant prayer held high that rod
Which threatens unbelievers with damned blood.
Perhaps 'twas solace through her djinn appeased,
Or counter to the logic Edwin trod,
But all the convert's fresh conviction seized
Her days, and shook the Book for all it could be squeezed.

XXXI

With plaintive, mellow lines the base of faith,
Her music filled cathedrals with its voice:
Each beat the pulse of God, each chord his breath,
Played 'gainst a choir or organ's solemn noise
As Joy, in satin gown, with careful poise,
Achieved a fame she'd never tried to win.
She wrote fresh music, biblical in choice,
A living sound to counter Mammon's din;
Yet wormed a pensive, sad reprise beneath her skin.

XXXII

Though fêted both by colleagues and by friends,
Though ringed by crowds who praised her as their own,
Inviting her to all the latest trends
(Ignoring those from which the bloom had flown),
She ever felt an exile and alone;
A fierce, tempestuous fire welled from her core–
The counterpoint to all she had outgrown.
She poured her heart in one great cello score:
It celebrated faith, yet wanted something more.

In Music's Power

XXXIII

For faith requires unquestioned certainty,
Yet certainty had seeped from her crushed vase,
With bruised love shielded from her enmity
So abyss-deep it never gave her cause
To think it still within, or question Cupid's laws.
Likewise, her cello concerto remained
Unfinished – hidden, like mist-shrouded moors;
The beauty and the power it contained
Were lost while rooted passion was by doubt restrained.

XXXIV

Edwin, meanwhile, had finished all his tasks;
His work with Cheryl finally was done.
He'd looked at Nature through a hundred masks,
Each showing where some battle had been won.
Cosmology had pushed him from the sun
To utmost reaches of the Universe;
He'd seen life, through his good viderium,
Burst forth from chemicals to fill Earth's purse
With life-forms up to man – God's gift and Nature's curse.

XXXV

He'd stripped computers bare to naked boards
Subpopulated by atomic switch,
With microprocessors as logic swords
To number-crunch a swathe through complex hitch
While binding modern life with data stitch.
His world spun – girdled by a web of wire;
Nostalgically, he thought it more a witch
That's best consumed on golden age's fire,
But all his learning could not set ablaze that pyre.

Girders in the Sand

XXXVI

But as he learnt, he found undrempt of gaps
Within the core of knowledge he'd accrued.
No sums can calculate a lover's lapse,
Nor know the tumbling orbits of the asteroid brood;
And 'probability' steers atoms, glued
Together in a hazy quark-soup core;
For chaos rules the detail and destroys the mood
Which Cheryl set from Newton's simple law:
All certainty of God is hid for evermore.

XXXVII

Two separate lives, by golden band conjoined,
One common mass in orbit circled round
The child, whose selfless love Joy had purloined,
And distant space the void where passion drowned.
And mutual friends looked on this dreadful ground
And stood unsure: to speak in plea of peace,
Or shuffle by, lest nervous glance astound
The one, or startle like the watchful geese
Which cackle danger, till complicit yearning cease.

XXXVIII

So might have jigged for ever this cleft pair,
Had not the unknown fate perturbed their plain.
With sudden shock of glazed and vacant stare,
The child grew ill, through fever of the brain,
Was carried to an over-known domain,
Familiar in his eye as his old room:
The paediatric ward, where long she'd lain
When he'd first rushed to her as severed groom
To forge parental bonds from blind genetic loom.

XXXIX

For days in stupor, marble-still and white,
She unresponsive lay as salt dripped in
And carried nourishment, and drugs to fight
By ceaseless chemistry the foe within.
Cachectic grew her waist, her cheek elfin,
With little sign encouraging less hope.
So still she lay, as Edwin brushed her skin
With trembling hand, upon the deathward slope,
Held there, twixt empty life and death, by prayer's slim rope.

XL

Then on the Sunday, as she lay, Joy brought
Respite and made the vigil compromise,
Whilst Mary-Anne slept on, in comma caught
Beyond all whispered comfort or surmise.
Joy moistened lips and wiped the brow and eyes,
She squeezed her hand and groomed the matted hair
With inner strength, which trusting faith supplies,
And fetched her cello with its soulful air,
To which piercing refrain at last the child did stir.

XLI

Life grows in many forms of diverse hues
Which range from roseate to Arctic ice,
Yet rarely take the shape a man might choose.
A child's sickbed must grow a subtle spice
To draw this flavour, friendship, from such mice;
Bacteria and circumstance combined,
Confounding Einstein, acting as God's dice
To bring two lives together from their bind:
The one to music wed, the other science-splined.

Girders in the Sand

XLII

They talked of times they'd shared before they'd wed:
Of moments touched by tenderness and hope;
A future stretched before them, clear ahead,
A new and empty stage, yet full of scope,
Upon which– free of trouble– they'd elope
To jounce and sing before they grew alone;
Of how, apart, each one had learnt to cope;
How, secretly, each touched the Brontë stone;
Of how they'd each seen places, once together known.

XLIII

With each breath building strength the next to forge,
Upon the child hope fluttered like a robe
Until her defervescence crossed the gorge
Dividing life from form upon this globe.
Across the bed, they touched, each separate lobe
United by their fear and stark relief.
They did not kiss – Joy balked at that sharp probe –
But side by side they smiled at fleeing grief,
And parleyed for a friendship, forgiving love's cruel thief.

XLIV

With grey, wild hair and probing, saddened eyes,
And hands, enlarged by burden of much pain,
Which swept great arcs through wisdom's cloudy skies,
The old neurologist, who loved the brain,
Declared that, though she live, the child might wane
Through damaged intellect; but on each day,
As Edwin talked, Joy played and sang again
Until the child's eyes brightened– full of play
And throwing the good doctor into disarray.

XLV

That night when silence filled a world in sleep–
As cooling cat's-paws brush a breathless pond
To stir the stillness of the hidden deep–
The girl awoke as to a magic wand,
And stretched in bed, weak as a lily frond.
Such rampant joy can none but sufferers know:
The music maker's gigue and sarabande,
The gardener's delight in rose and hoe,
The parents' peace of mind from lamentation's woe.

XLVI

Though languid in her frame, her mind was strong
As daily, on the dot of ten past four,
Down corridors they chaired her, out among
The stroke victims, for physio on the floor,
Till soon she hobbled through the wide ward door
Unaided, but for sticks to steady gait.
Her spindled arms and wizened legs were straw;
With looks like Lowry's figures in The Tate,
She made Joy promise that they'd never separate.

XLVII

For her security, a chair of chrome
Was leant to ride the streets. Then she, death past,
Upon the passing of a week, went home–
Her limbs fleshed out, her sticks aside now cast.
Joy touched the door of Edwin's house aghast,
But would not venture in– until the child,
Ashake and trembling, screamed a loud lambast:
"You promised to return! I've been beguiled!"
Her whole demeanour, though still weak, lacked manner mild.

Girders in the Sand

XLVIII

Full circle twice had Edwin travelled round,
Unearthing Nature's Laws with physics' rules.
He'd chased all knowledge to its highest ground;
Outlined the universe with cosmic tools
In measured microseconds as it cools;
Explored mutation's random walk to man
From microbes, through the life in salt rock pools;
Held faith in quantized quarks for atom's plan;
And all that can be known of how this world began.

XLIX

But through this search he'd naught of Heaven found,
Whose origins lay locked in barren law,
Invariably set as waves that pound
Cliff rocks to sand upon a lonely shore.
One steadfast thought became his clutching straw
And stopped his learning making total loss;
It moved as music had just once before
When he'd first loved, then known love's wretched cross:
Complexity emergent from primal chaos.

L

And from this bruisèd state Joy leant him strength
To sit awhile, recovering his poise
Until, armed by her faith, he came at length
To postulate those questions asked by boys:
Where is the God of might, of battle's noise;
Where does he now reside, with churches gone?
Where now the miracles which he employs,
When rational thought snuffs out the light he shone?
Thus grew the task he vowed to set his mind upon.

In Music's Power

LI

Through passing weeks, a harmony evolved
Whereby each, *Art* and *Science*, circled round
On civil words, remaining unconvolved.
In Edwin's home, Joy bowed her cello sound;
Subsuming to her score wild nature's ground,
She drained fresh knowledge with a drunkard's thirst,
Rewriting her concerto to confound
By juxtaposing ersatz themes she'd cursed,
Pitching a second cello to augment the first.

LII

That first was spirit – Ariel in flight,
Tone radiant and pure, its soaring beat
Distinguishing dark thought from fairer light
And lamping like bright hellion cold to heat;
Ephemeral, ascending scales so fleet
Gainst solid rocks of orchestrated chords,
They seemed to mount forever Heaven's seat.
Its bearing all the while inferred her Lord's
Until it fell in blood on sharp tympanic swords.

LIII

Now percolating quietness appeared
(Whose noble stillness inner ears might fill);
Slow threads reverberant which disappeared.
Uplifting silences, each vacuum still,
These hollow struts to sound gave added thrill
As though a mighty god would soon be slayed;
Interpolated, half-imagined notes, until–
Before discordant onslaughts wildly played–
With melancholic voice, the spritely thread decayed.

Girders in the Sand

LIV

Unnoticed, starting late, the second voice
Against the whole ensemble pitched its key:
Insistent, fixed, until there was no choice
But modulate this wild and wind swept tree,
As men escaping storms seek mountain's lee.
But even as the other fell in line,
The second cello moved to disagree
By cracking the harmonic woodwind shrine
With pizzicato chords in cascades plucked to shine.

LV

In recapitulation crept the first,
Its softly glowing colours building through
To lead the orchestration from the worst
Discordant pain. On notes of hope they flew,
Until the second's awful grieving grew
Subdued, to re-emerge in harmony;
Though rainbows' vivid lights from red to blue
Display their inner law in gaudy ray,
The brightest light is forged when all build glowing day.

LVI

Subconscious substance swelled within her heart:
This was her theme and– with completion– fame;
These two conjoined, now more than either part,
Touched undiscovered pastures and new game.
As eager batons rose to swell her name,
She turned to Edwin, child-like, weak and lost,
And clutched him as a stick to help the lame.
Bewildered by uncertainty's bleak frost,
They kissed– for love and art lack logic's stern riposte.

In Music's Power

LVII

That day, upon the merging of their selves,
Eternal laws were damned as thoughts best slain;
Replacing heavy books upon their shelves
He gave up further studies in disdain.
He'd watched each neurone pulse within the brain,
And knew that more than drops make mountain streams;
He'd reckoned all the forces in a crane
And calculated shear in bending beams–
Yet nothing knew of love content, or poets' dreams.

LVIII

As merged their bodies, and as friendship wants,
So merged their minds, each than before more strong.
For Joy, the hurt of music– art that haunts–
Grew firmer in fresh-loved Creation's song;
While Edwin, so engulfed by Nature's tongue,
Could view the world anew through dreaming slumber.
Through Joy, he learnt that sterile laws are wrong:
That mystery of life lies not in number,
But in complexity– from mankind grows the wonder.

LIX

Conforming to her faith, he studied prayer,
Re-reading ancient, gruesome texts of law–
Of God Creator, bidding man, "Beware!
Beware! I was and will be evermore.
Beware! No rival images adore.
Beware!– the wailing pit and waiting flame.
In faith believe, now question never more.
What man shall dare defy my hidden name?
Before creation I, the true Creator, came."

Girders in the Sand

LX

Yet restless grew his heart upon the day,
When he recalled the knowledge he'd hard won.
This primal God used simple chants to sway
His followers, and miracles to stun
Incredulous belief without question–
With more of magic than integrity.
Must all man's learning stop before begun,
With ignorance disguised as piety,
Or could God's thoughts be held with true sobriety?

LXI

Autumnal leaves slid slowly past his pane
Whilst humid, leaden air clung to his brow
And idleness lay heavy as a chain.
The oily river's glide beneath the bough
Drained, more than watered, parched fields put to plough.
A lonely swan, agrieving for her mate,
Would take no bread, nor any help allow,
But drifted as the current bore her fate;
So Edwin brooded as he turned to contemplate.

LXII

Through all his search, one question, "What is man?"
Had been repeated like a long refrain.
With Cheryl blindly stumbling, "What is man?"
Had wrenched him from complacent counterpane.
Now pushed he through the darkness once again,
Repeating oft the question he had posed
In restless hope of insights to attain
That revelations, yet to be exposed,
Might in his brain fresh flower, to him alone disclosed.

In Music's Power

LXIII

He ran to Cheryl, pleading for her help;
This boy who'd been her head-high acolyte
Now simpered like a tail-down beaten whelp.
She'd been to him a mentor, guide and light,
Concealing nothing– plain or recondite.
Arrayed in red she spun her paradigm;
Both arrogant and proud from learning's height–
Which vests in *Sapiens* its patronym–
She outlined once again the distant heaven's rim.

LXIV

First, formless heat– intensity beyond
All mathematicians' powers to quantify–
Spread uniformly, smoother than a pond,
From which surprising particles defy
Proud atom-smashers' work, and mystify.
Yet from this searing maelstrom issued sprays
Of nucleons, with weight to dignify
These baryonic remnants, from whose haze
Came fuel to set like dust the gathering stars ablaze.

LXV

There, deep within those fiery furnaces,
Against all probability, were brewed
Those metals which mankind still burnishes
For ornament or nuclear fuel. They spewed
Out from the bursting globes as if imbued
With inner meaning, yet to be declared:
Uranium and gold, and diamonds crude,
Whose proto-crystals all remained unpaired
Until in planetary discs their brilliance flared.

Girders in the Sand

LXVI

Now complexed carbon bangs the lifeless stage
In dancing permutations beyond count;
Wild molecules, improbable to gauge,
In pounding, wild seas, till their amount
Builds self-sustaining chains to form the fount
Of living forms. These primal crypto-cells
Competitively obstacles surmount
Until their number, like some virus, swells;
Within tight synergistic membranes each one dwells.

LXVII

What creature first trudged from the single-celled?
No eye could ken wild evolution's break,
But from these burst diversity, which swelled
Beyond imagining. Green plants to shake
Foundations more than rupturing earthquake.
New species thrived in air of oxygen,
Then spawned to drum the early earth awake;
Great beds of chalk and limestone were laid then,
Accumulating finally the bones of men.

LXVIII

Whether by chance, or by Creator's plan,
Or some watchmaker operating blind
To build from neural nets the brain of man,
However self-awareness is defined,
Self-thought implies complexity of mind.
But not *pre hoc* analysis nor contumely
Could predict thought once neural cells combined;
For language, art, music and poetry,
Like love, require a shared existence to run free.

LXIX

At this, Cheryl's didacticism stopped.
She'd brought him from Big Bang to social law
By analytic steps which wildly loped,
Yet each one built upon the one before.
Where logic permeates into the core,
Divinity and purpose hold no place;
His question, "What is man?" now asked once more
Returned but silence, and a blank averted face;
But of a God, of any sort, there was no trace.

LXX

Then Cheryl spun to glare at him and said,
"You whimper like some pup that's wet the floor;
Who spring from nothing, nothing are when dead.
You've glimpsed man's total knowledge through my door;
What you seek lies beyond this teacher's roar—
Beyond, perhaps, all knowledge on this sphere;
Now turn away and look at me no more.
You need the council of a mystic seer,
Some desert-dwelling hermit and his life austere."

LXXI

What will impels the questing man to roam;
What pleasure, craft or book might sound a start,
Tempting the fancy to abandon home
For hermeneutic life, from love apart?
What lonely hour may drive the aching heart
To take no more than fortune for a guide,
To seize with eagerness the unfilled chart
And sweet, familiar comfort cast aside,
While equilibrating friends condemn his arrant pride?

Girders in the Sand

LXXII

The silent, lonely emptiness was tart;
His anguish Joy could not alleviate,
Nor comprehend the hollow in his heart.
His quest verged him to self-exterminate
To learn what world, past death, hid desolate.
Through moaning torment, his hand stayed the knife,
Full knowing corpses don't communicate.
Self-pity filled each day his wretched life,
Distracting beyond reason's bond his caring wife.

LXXIII

Than to be loved, to love is greater far.
Love scorches futile cords with proud disdain;
By love's resolve we hazard for a star;
And yet, we know love free from hurt is vain—
What love is great, that has no bond in pain?
The loving mother will her life devote
To dying child, one moment more to gain;
For love of us, Christ shed his manly coat;
For love, the sweet musician plucks her fitful note.

LXXIV

Alcestis-like, Joy pondered long if she
Could take his place and herself immolate.
Despairing least barbed doubt pricked him to flee,
Her bitterness at love's betrayed estate
Took her beyond all rational debate.
A perched piano, wedged atop a peg,
She set with suicidal thought its weight,
Then kicked it, leaving free her jutting leg
As it crashed down with thunderous roar like powder keg.

In Music's Power

LXXV

In dreams she came to him, through death she spoke;
A living form now caged within his head,
Whose presence plagued him as each day awoke.
No fire could more intensely weld his dread
Than this strange act: to self-kill in his stead.
With gashing time, the visions grew more stark,
Her voice as clear as if she were undead;
Then, like some new-lit lamp, she torched the dark,
Replacing doubt with hard-won faith and joyful spark.

LXXVI

God lives not in man's origin or start,
But on a future path we've yet to steer;
When God squats at our birth, we draw apart,
But God who's at our end will draw us near.
As minds in isolation disappear,
Combined in all the minds that yet will be
And all that were since man did first appear;
A web of unsurpassed complexity
Has generated, beyond man, a deity,

LXXVII

A God emergent, not in any plan,
Now grown beyond imagining's confines,
In whom, potential once in the Big Bang,
Invigorated nothingness now shines.
In this dim realm, humanity combines
As single cells complete the living whole;
Our telescopes look back in vain for signs—
Pure thought takes on the mantle of the soul.
Beyond our lives God lies: the last, though unseen, goal.

Girders in the Sand

New Dawn

By sudden death he lay subdued;
For with Joy's swift, mind-melting scream
Died god: the god of ancient ways,
The god of primal held belief,
The god of ritual and dance,
The god creator, the all-wise,
The all-pervading reckoner.

To peer at distant deities,
He'd held too long the telescope
Reversed, its image small.
Now God emergent towered near:
Within his head, his thoughts, his hopes,
Yet web-like spun by all mankind.
Far larger than a single death,
Far greater than a brief man's life,
Out looming with a sudden blaze
To rip the misty morning haze
And lend uncertain future hope.
These laws were set when time began,
Like girders in the sand.

Mankind will strive to fathom more
By taking meliorism's door,
And step beyond this cloying earth
To touch the stars by this God's birth.

Emergent Power

O Power, emergent from the mind of man,
Existing by our blocks of tumbling thought,
Yet powerful as God of the Koran
Or Christian deity from Yahweh wrought;
Evolving Power, in future locked, not past,
God each to Heathen, Hindu, Tao or Jew,
Yet limitless, as cells were once surpassed
By creatures who their forebears never knew;
Help us attain the summit of your way,
To trust your purpose, and conceive our own.
Beyond the idle moments of each day,
Your essence shapes us as the weathered stone.

This summer's bloom on lustrous fortune's hill
Shall overcome discordant winter's chill.

* * * * *

So ends our story, and our rhyme,
Brave attempts to compact time,
Where art and science merge.
Now greater minds must contemplate
Emergent power's growing state,
To stand on future's verge.